Reading the
Liturgy

Reading the Liturgy

An Exploration of Texts in Christian Worship

Juliette J. Day

BLOOMSBURY

LONDON • NEW DELHI • NEW YORK • SYDNEY

Bloomsbury T&T Clark

An imprint of Bloomsbury Publishing Plc

50 Bedford Square	1385 Broadway
London	New York
WC1B 3DP	NY 10018
UK	USA

www.bloomsbury.com

Bloomsbury is a registered trade mark of Bloomsbury Publishing Plc

First published 2014

© Juliette J. Day, 2014

British Library Cataloguing-in-Publication Data
A catalogue record for this book is available from the British Library.

ISBN: HB: 978-0-5671-3328-1
PB: 978-0-5670-6335-9
ePDF: 978-0-5674-2526-3
ePub: 978-0-5672-2013-4

Library of Congress Cataloging-in-Publication Data
Day, Juliette J.
Reading the Liturgy / Juliette J. Day p.cm
Includes bibliographic references and index.
ISBN 978-0-5671-3328-1 (hardcover)

Typeset by Newgen Knowledge Works (P) Ltd., Chennai, India
Printed and bound in Great Britain

CONTENTS

LIST OF ILLUSTRATIONS

Figure

Tables

ACKNOWLEDGEMENTS

Excerpts from the English translation of *The Roman Missal* © 2010, International Commission on English in the Liturgy Corporation (ICEL); excerpts from the English translation of *Eucharistic Prayers for Masses with Children* © 2013, ICEL. All rights reserved.

Excerpt from the *Iona Abbey Worship Book* © 2001, Wild Goose Publications, Glasgow.

Extracts from The Book of Common Prayer, the rights in which are vested in the Crown, are reproduced by permission of the Crown's Patentee, Cambridge University Press.

Extracts from *The Alternative Service Book* are copyright © The Archbishops' Council, 1980 and are reproduced by permission.

Extracts from *Common Worship: Services and Prayers* are copyright © The Archbishops' Council, 2000 and are reproduced by permission. All rights reserved. <copyright@churchofengland.org>

Excerpt from the hymn 'God of Concrete, God of Steel' by Richard G. Jones, reproduced by permission of Stainer & Bell Ltd, London, England. <www.stainer.co.uk>

ABBREVIATIONS

ANF	A. C. Coxe, James Donaldson, and Alexander Roberts (eds), *The Ante-Nicene Fathers: Translations of the Writings of the Fathers Down to A.D. 325* (repr. Grand Rapids, MI: Eerdmans, 1985)
ASB	*The Alternative Service Book*
BCP	The Book of Common Prayer
CW	*Common Worship: Services and Prayers for the Church of England*
CWCI	*Common Worship: Christian Initiation*
CWPS	*Common Worship: Pastoral Services*
JAAR	*The Journal of the American Academy of Religion*
JTS	*The Journal of Theological Studies*
MC	*Mystagogical Catecheses* attributed to Cyril of Jerusalem
OCA	Orientalia Christiana Analecta
OCP	*Orientalia Analecta Periodica*
OrChr	*Oriens Christianus*
TS	*Theological Studies*
TU	Texte und Unterschungen
ZKG	*Zeitschrift für Kirchengeschichte*

INTRODUCTION

Look again at the front cover. We see four groups of liturgical participants with a richly covered coffin in the centre. We see them praying, reading and possibly singing. If we are familiar with the style of picture and the type of activity it displays, we can see that they are medieval, that the image comes from a manuscript miniature and that this would seem to be a funeral mass for a wealthy and prestigious person. But if we look again, we can see that the coffin is the focus of only one group; the rest read, speak and sing from the liturgical books before them and pay no heed to either the deceased or the principal mourners, nor even to each other. The painter of this image intends us to understand what is happening here by reference to the coffin first, but secondly by the texts which constitute the means of active participation by the clergy and choir; however, at first glance we may have not noticed the texts despite the best efforts of the picture editor to highlight them. What is ironic is that if the cover had depicted a contemporary act of worship, our attention may have been drawn to the people and the place, to the purpose of the liturgical action, but probably not to the books and leaflets held in the hands of the participants or stacked up in front of them in the pew or on the altar. It is as if the liturgical texts are the 'elephant in the church' – we rely on them for the conduct of our worship, for the language of our prayers, as the means of sacramental encounter with God, even for what we should do, where, when and how in the service, but are reluctant to 'see' them when engaged in the worship of God.

The purpose of this book is to force us to 'see' the texts and to investigate how their textuality functions in the liturgical act in the ways just summarized, and also how their very textuality generates a particular type of meaning-making independent of the ritual context. In much of the modern world, worshippers are also readers and being so, they have a well-developed, yet implicit, set of literacy skills which they do not abandon at the church door. So, in order to 'see' the texts, we shall 'read the liturgy'. In the chapters which follow we investigate different aspects of textuality which are implicit in the production and use of liturgical texts, as they are in all texts, through the insights gathered from a range of contemporary literary, linguistic and philosophical theories applied to specific historic and modern liturgical texts and scholarship.

The liturgical texts of our own Christian tradition are naturally the ones that spring to mind when we start to see and read them, and thus some may find rather too much emphasis upon examples drawn from my English Anglican background. This bias is not intended to make any particular claims for the textual tradition of that church, but, simply, the examples proved useful for the points I wished to make. Readers of this book are very much encouraged to consider their familiar texts in light of the theoretical perspectives and preliminary conclusions offered here, and it is very much my intention to provoke further scholarly and pastoral discussion of them.

1

Text

Our churches and our worship are text-bound. If we want to know when the service is, we are more likely to look for text on a sign or website than listen out for the ringing of a bell; when we enter a church, its character and activities are displayed on signboards, and then when entering the worship space itself we will, more often than not, be handed a hymn book and if not a prayer book then at least a leaflet containing selected texts to be spoken during worship and some rudimentary directions. Worship is constructed from books – missals, lectionaries, sacramentaries, hymnals, bibles, even text projected onto screens; the internet as well has increased opportunities for worship by providing online versions of the daily office which is identical to the printed text but in a new media. The worship event consists of texts arranged and spoken according to established patterns, sometimes accompanied by rituals which also have textual authority.

In the worship event, at least in churches with authorized liturgical texts, ministers and people *read* the liturgy – worship consists of a period of particular text-based activities. Despite the 'nose in the book' manner in which much worship is conducted, participants will be averse to calling their activity 'reading aloud to God' and are more likely to emphasize the entire ritual event as encounter with God which is made possible primarily through speech. With liturgical texts more than others, then, the relationship between speech and written text needs to be explored and further what distinguishes a speaker from a reader and even from a worshipper. In this chapter, I will establish some key features of a liturgical text such that in the subsequent chapters we can turn our attention to the production and interpretation of these texts and how that affects what worshippers do with them in the liturgical event.

A brief history of liturgical texts

Worshippers prioritize speech over written text as the effective component of their activity. This, in part, is related to the historical development of Christian liturgy as well as to concepts around the scriptures (written) being the word (spoken) of God and the priority given to the inspired speech of prophets in both Testaments.[1] For Christians, then, there is the paradox of asserting the primacy of speech communication, but conveying that through text. This is the case in liturgy too. Our first evidence for liturgical forms is in texts which assert that worship is not conducted by text, but by the leader using what words he chooses and to the best of his ability. This very familiar account of a Christian assembly from Justin Martyr makes the point clearly:

> And on the day called Sunday, all who live in cities or in the country gather together to one place, and the memoirs of the apostles or the writings of the prophets are read, as long as time permits; then, when the reader has ceased, the president verbally instructs, and exhorts to the imitation of these good things. Then we all rise together and pray, and, as we before said, when our prayer is ended, bread and wine and water are brought, and the president in like manner offers prayers and thanksgivings, according to his ability, and the people assent, saying Amen; and there is a distribution to each, and a participation of that over which thanks have been given . . .[2]

It would be difficult to discern the precise point at which liturgy became textual. Early 'sacramentaries', such as that of Serapion, which we will examine in the next chapter, show that at least one bishop in the early decades of the fourth century found it

---

[1] See, for example, Paul's injunctions on prophecy in 1 Thessalonians 14, also in early Christian documents such as *Didache* 10.

[2] Justin Martyr, *Apology* I, 67 (*ANF*, vol. 1, p. 186).

helpful to have a written collection of the prayers he needed to fulfil his liturgical duties. Additionally, church orders such as the *Didascalia Apostolorum*, the *Apostolic Tradition* and the *Apostolic Constitutions* indicate that there was a market for manuals to guide liturgical worship as well as other aspects of community life.[3] The move to text, though, was not inevitable. During the fourth and fifth centuries, the episcopate attracted highly educated men who were famed for their rhetorical skills like Basil of Caesarea, Gregory Nazianzus, Ambrose of Milan and Augustine of Hippo, for whom eloquent and fluent public speech without a text was the hallmark of their craft. Sermons of the finest preachers were taken down in shorthand as they were preached and then would be refined by the preacher for collation and circulation, but the evidence for this happening to liturgical texts is non-existent.[4] If anything, liturgical texts begin as an *aide-mémoire* prior to the liturgical event and not a record of it afterwards, and this can be seen especially in the Western and Roman church which developed a tradition of variable thematic introductions to the Eucharistic prayer which otherwise contained a fixed sequence of topics. The creativity of the Roman bishops, especially, can be seen in the early sacramentaries where multiple prefaces and collects for each Sunday and feast of the year were collected together from *libelli*, or pamphlets, preserved in the Lateran library.[5] Although the contents of these sacramentaries clearly reveal that they were composed by different authors, some of whom can be clearly identified on stylistic grounds, either the *libelli* did not preserve the name or the compilers did not think it important to attach names to them. These sacramentaries are, though, simply compendiums and not books for use in the liturgy; their arrangement and variety indicate that they were intended to provide models for bishops and priests who would still be expected to improvise. This is evident even in the late fifth century as we can

---

[3]For more on these church orders as a genre see, Paul Bradshaw, *The Search for the Origins of Christian Worship Sources and Methods for the Study of Early Liturgy* (2nd ed. London: SPCK, 2002), chapter 4.

[4]See Mary B. Cunningham and Pauline Allen (eds), *Preacher and Audience: Studies in Early Christian and Byzantine Homiletics* (Leiden: Brill, 1998), pp. 11–12.

[5]See, for example, the so-called Gelasian sacramentary. Text and studies in Leo Eizenhöfer, Petrus Siffrin and L. C. Mohlberg, *Liber Sacramentorum Romanae Aeclesiae Ordinis Anni Circuli* (Cod. Vat. Reg. Lat. 316/ Paris Bibl. Nat. 7193, 41/56) (*Sacramentarium Gelasianum*) (Rome: Herder, 1960).

see in Gregory of Tours' (538–94) praise for Sidonius Apollonaris, Bishop of Clermont Ferrand (d. c. 487):

> The holy Sidonius was so eloquent that he generally improvised what he wished to say without any hesitation and in the clearest manner. And it happened one day that he went by invitation to a fête at the church of the monastery which we have mentioned before, and when his book, by which he had been wont to celebrate the holy services, was maliciously taken away, he went through the whole service of the fête improvising with such readiness that he was admired by all, and it was believed by the bystanders that it was not a man who had spoken there but an angel.[6]

Although clearly not an eyewitness account, it does indicate how much the oral was prized even if it was accepted that some text was required.

Authoritative liturgical texts emerge alongside the consolidation of episcopal, and especially papal, power. The 'Book of Pontiffs' (*Liber Pontificalis*) makes several anachronistic references to papal authority for the introduction of liturgical units into what the compilers presumed was a pre-existing text; however, it is in relation to the liturgical reforms of Gregory I (c. 540–604) that personal, liturgical and textual authority come together. Gregory himself notes that the Canon of the Mass was compiled by a *scholasticus* (scribe) sometime before his election:[7] this presumes liturgical performance based on authoritative texts. Liturgical reforms from then on are text-based: Charlemagne sends to Pope Hadrian for an authoritative sacramentary to provide the basis for his reforms in 785–6; among the Protestant reformers Cranmer's express aim was to provide one book for the whole country; the Council of Trent abolished all but the most ancient liturgical texts in preference to the one approved there. A counter-move among some reform movements is also evident in the return to oral composition

---

[6]Gregory of Tours, *History of the Franks* 2.22. English translation in Ernest Brehaut, *Gregory of Tours: History of the Franks* (New York: Norton, 1969). <http://www.fordham.edu/halsall/basis/gregory-hist.asp#book3> [accessed 27 March 2012].

[7]Gregory the Great, *Epistle* 9, 26. See John R. C. Martyn, *The Letters of Gregory the Great*, vol. 2 (Toronto: Pontifical Institute of Mediaeval Studies, 2004), pp. 561–3.

in worship, although even here the abolition of liturgical texts only served to assert the primacy of the biblical text.

Once text-based liturgy becomes normative, the exponential growth of different liturgical books seems to have followed soon after. There are books of antiphons for the choir, of gospels for the deacons, office books for monks, pontificals for bishops.[8] The multiplication of liturgical books is related to the multiplication of ministries in the church and, just as they undoubtedly assisted the efficient conduct of worship, they were also indicators of status when only those authorized to use a particular book owned or had access to it. Even today, Roman Catholic and Anglican deacons receive a book of gospels at ordination as a sign of their authority to read the gospel in the liturgy. The laity, too, were not immune from a text-based prayer life: Books of Hours contained shortened offices taken from the monastic context and were the foundation of domestic piety for a certain class, primarily of women, for whom the possession of a richly illuminated book was a status symbol. Images in such books of a woman, often the recipient, seated at prayer using the very same book that she has in her hands vividly assert the primacy of text and reading in private as well as public worship.[9] It is in light of this multiplicity of books, ministries and 'liturgical power' that Cranmer's radical and democratizing one-volume Book of Common Prayer should be considered.

After the decisive shift from oral to written liturgical texts, the next great upheaval was the invention of printing which permitted a greater number of people to have access to the books and to a large extent removed the imprecision caused by inaccurate copying which was a feature of manuscripts. Between then and the last twenty years, the only comparable change is in electronic publishing and internet

---

[8]The standard studies of these are in Cyrille Vogel, *Medieval Liturgy: An Introduction to the Sources* (Washington, DC: Pastoral Press, 1986) and Eric Palazzo, *A History of Liturgical Books: From the Beginning to the Thirteenth Century* (Collegeville: Liturgical Press, c. 1998).

[9]The owners were also encouraged to imitate the prayer life of Mary by images of the Annunciation in which Mary is depicted seated with a book of hours on her lap as she is interrupted by Gabriel. For an example see a French Book of Hours from c. 1500 in the Bodleian Library at the University of Oxford (MS. Buchanan e. 3) at <http://www.bodley.ox.ac.uk/dept/scwmss/wmss/medieval/jpegs/buchanan/e/1000/00300013.jpg> [accessed 19 August 2013]. Also, Janet Backhouse, *Illumination from Books of Hours* (London: British Library, 2004).

resources, but the impact of that on liturgical texts and on worship
has still to be worked out. It could be said though that this new
media has highlighted the ephemeral nature of much liturgical text.
Liturgical texts are collected together Sunday by Sunday, printed
on a leaflet handed out before worship and recycled immediately
after. The return of the *libellus* perhaps! The scraps of early prayer
formulae have only been uncovered by chance discoveries in monastic
libraries, the Canon put together by a Roman *scholasticus*, and even
the impractical books listed by Cranmer have disappeared.[10] Once
a liturgical text has no use in a worship event it is soon discarded
and replaced by a current one. Paul Bradshaw emphasized what
liturgical texts share with some other types of texts, especially those
intended for performance (i.e. Shakespeare's plays), that the content
does not remain fixed for all time. To this genre he gave the name
'living literature', which is identified by 'the fact that it circulated
within a community, forming a part of its heritage and tradition, but
underwent periodic revision and rewriting in response to changing
historical and cultural circumstances'.[11] This is a process which may
affect contemporary texts just as much as it seems to be displayed
by historic liturgical texts but, also, we shall argue in the remainder
of this book, liturgical texts share textual features evident in all
texts. To prepare for those investigations, though, we first need to
establish what we mean by 'text'.

What is a text?

Etymologically, 'text' (Latin: *textus*) is something which is woven
together, and this observation has proved useful in recent discussions
of what a text is as it draws our attention not just to an object,
but to the product of an activity. It also forces us to think of the
composite nature of the product, a weaving together of different
verbal elements to produce a new 'thing'.

---

[10]In the preface to the 1549 BCP, Cranmer asserts the practical benefits of having
only one book by listing a range of liturgical books which it replaced; these books
cannot all be clearly identified because they no longer exist.
[11]Paul Bradshaw, 'Liturgy and "Living Literature"', in Paul Bradshaw and Bryan
Spinks (eds), *Liturgy in Dialogue: Essays in Memory of Ronald Jasper* (London:
SPCK, 1993), p. 138.

A text exists at the surface, that is the page, or book, or scrap of paper. It is constituted by words placed in connection to each other so as to produce potentially meaningful units. The means of production characteristic of a text is writing, inscriptions of symbols (letters) on a page; this act of writing endues a thought or speech with the potential for permanence, or may even replace speech entirely. A written word need not be remembered because it can be returned to for as long as the text which contains it exists. Writing, and therefore text production, is a purposed activity, it requires an intention to commit to a permanent form. The words of speech disappear as soon as they are spoken as Walter Ong so memorably put it, 'When I pronounce the word "permanence", by the time I get to the "-nence", the "perma-" is gone and has to be gone.'[12] The recall of speech is left to chance, whereas a text is theoretically always open to the possibility of immediate retrieval.

Although I have suggested that a text is the product of an activity, at the point of reception that activity is masked, indeed it is normal to read a text oblivious of the producer, her drafts and the staring into space hunting for the next word or phrase. Once produced, a text has a life of its own which just as often as not relates to other texts as to the world. It cannot, like speech, clarify in different words what the author meant to say and its interpretation is dependent upon the reader. The fixity of the form, that is the visual and physical inscription of words, does not imply fixity of meaning, so the text is always the location of a series of transactions. The transaction between author and reader can only take place at the surface level, but its meaning is only generated by the transactions between the text and the reader, by the text and all other texts known by the reader. This naturally gives rise to a potentially limitless number of interpretations, and that requires us to dispense with the notion of a text as an authoritative repository of meaning.

What can be designated 'text' may not be determined by quantity, media or quality. 'Text' can be used in general and specific senses, as a singular, plural or uncountable. A library contains text in a generic sense, some text as opposed to all the text in the world, as well as the particular texts I wish to consult. Usually when I use 'text', I make an assumption that the reader, or listener, and I

---

share an understanding about what is meant – most often the text physically before us as the subject of our conversation. Its ability to indicate specific objects as well as a general phenomenon alerts us to the fluidity with which the term is most often used, and this of course is problematic when trying to separate the specific from the general in a more analytical way. In contemporary linguistics and philosophy, definitions of 'text' have sought to distinguish between the object and the process, to explore the writtenness of text in relation to speech, and to find a way by which process, product and reception could be integrated into a coherent formulation. Thus for example, Roland Barthes distinguished between the 'work', that is the finished object which occupies a physical space, from 'text' as 'a methodological field': 'the work can be held in the hand, the text is held in language, [it] only exists in the movement of a discourse.'[13] The text never exhausts its meanings, it constantly offers new ones, 'the stereographic plurality of its weave of signifiers', whereas the work is only 'moderately symbolic (its symbolic runs out, comes to a halt)', it is closed.[14] Barthes, Julia Kristeva and the deconstructionists remove 'text' from the physical object to a process of signification which is greater than writing on a page. This is at some distance from where I began this section, and may not be immediately helpful for our project, but it is useful in showing how abstract and dynamic notions of 'text' can be, especially when they force us to attend to how meaning is generated and the interconnectedness of texts, in contrast to the rather static notion which both liturgists and worshippers tend to have of them.

More useful, perhaps, are those studies which investigate the relationship of the spoken to the written in the text. Ferdinand de Saussure in his pioneering, but now highly challenged, *Course in General Linguistics* articulated the relationship between them. First he distinguished between language ('*langue*') a universal system of signs, and speech ('*parole*'), which could be expressed verbally or in writing:

> Language and writing are two distinct systems of signs: the second exists for the sole purpose of representing the first. The linguistic object is not both the written and the spoken forms of words; the

[13]Roland Barthes, 'From Work to Text', idem., *Image, Music, Text*, translated by Stephen Heath (London: Fontana Press, 1977), pp. 156–7.
[14]Ibid., p. 158.

spoken forms alone constitute the object. But the spoken word is so intimately bound to its written image that the latter manages to usurp the main role. People attach more importance to the written image of a vocal sign than to the sign itself.[15]

Here then there is an equality in the manner of expression, although speech is primary, both speech and writing stand in the same relationship to that which is to be expressed (the utterance or discourse).

Paul Ricoeur, who was not alone in critiquing this position, wished to make a clear distinction between what was spoken and what written: 'what is fixed by writing is a discourse which could be said but it is written precisely because it is not said'.[16] For him, writing occurs where speech could have occurred and thus it may replace speech or indeed be completely unrelated to speech. The link between speech and writing is purely the ability of writing to fix speech and make it available after the moment. Thus the text does not depend upon prior speech but upon the 'discourse', the message; the text is a means of preserving and transmitting the discourse. In the act of reading, the reader is reliant solely upon the text to uncover the meaning (referent) of the discourse, whereas in speech, the interlocutors will use physical and verbal signs to make the referent clear. In speech, we can interrogate, probe and challenge our interlocutor; when reading a text the author is not present, and thus revealing the referent is entirely a matter for the reader who will bring to the text all the experience and techniques at her disposal.

The final theoretical model I wish to consult is Walter Ong's discussion of orality and literacy in which he asserts that primary orality, exhibited in pre-literate cultures, is not available to literate cultures whose speech and thoughts are always conditioned by the experience of writing and the objectivity in relation to utterances that writing engenders. Citing Derrida, he comments that the

---

[15]Ferdinand De Saussure, *Course in General Linguistics*, [3rd ed. Charles Bally and Albert Reidlinger (eds); translated by Wade Baskin] (New York: Philosophical Library, 1959), pp. 23–4. <http://openlibrary.org/books/OL23291521M/Course_in_general_linguistics> [accessed 27 March 2012].

[16]Paul Ricoeur, 'What is a text?' idem., *From Text to Action: Essays in Hermeneutics II*, translated by Kathleen Blamey and John Thompson (London: Athlone Press, 1991), p. 106.

written word is not a real word but a sign, 'coded symbols', which
to the literate may evoke actual or imagined sound.[17] However,
reading is such an interiorized activity that literates no longer need
to articulate the words physically, we encounter text visually and
words cease to be strongly related to sound. Print, he argues, further
removes writing from speech by locking words into a position in
space, presenting them in an ordered and regular fashion which
facilitates rapid and thus silent reading.[18] 'Print reinforces the
sense of language as essentially textual. The printed text, not the
written text, is the text in its fullest, paradigmatic, form.'[19] Writing
and print could not be further from speech, the latter being clearly
undertaken by a living person with whom I have contact, while the
written word exists regardless of the mortality of the writer, and
so consequently the writer needs to exercise greater care because
his words will be interpreted in a context over which he has no
control.[20] So meaning must reside in the language as there is no
intonation, facial expression or gesture to make things clear. Once
produced, the text exists by itself and for itself; whereas speech is
always a relational activity.

These perspectives force us to concentrate on the relatedness of
speech communication and written communication, and in the case
of liturgical texts to consider how a primarily written text becomes
a speech event. It has also highlighted to us how the text needs to
be self-sufficient if it is to convey the author's meaning effectively,
but that in all cases the reader will apply their own criteria when
interpreting it. These ideas need to be borne in mind as we reflect
upon what a 'liturgical text' might be.

What is a liturgical text?

Liturgical worship is communal and oral. Worshippers relate to
each other physically through sense perceptions – sight, sound
and sometimes smell – and therefore some of the conditions for

---

[17]Ong, *Orality and Literacy*, p. 74.
[18]Ibid., pp. 119–20.
[19]Ibid., p. 128.
[20]Ibid., pp. 100–3.

orality, as Ong describes it, are met. However, the words uttered are scripted, written, printed and thus the text intrudes into an activity which does not by its nature require one. As Ong has shown, text, especially a printed text, creates distance between author and reader, it calls for an interiorized and private consumption of the text, it requires no specific context in which its meaning is revealed. Now we could argue that the liturgical text is quite distinct from other texts in that a specific context is required for it to be meaningful,[21] but the readers of this book will become only too aware that we can read liturgical texts outside the worship event. The results of that interpretation may be different, but the variation may not be more pronounced than that between different individuals during worship. Liturgical texts, though, do look like other texts, they are just words inscribed on a page and as we shall see in later chapters share features with many, if not all, other texts.

If we follow Ricour in relating the text to a discourse, then we may wish to consider whether, in expressing attitudes to and about God (our discourse), the liturgical text stands in an equal relationship to how we might express these things orally or is completely different. That is, does it matter if we say something from a text or without, as long as the content is the same? Or, is the writing and printing of text a fundamentally different thing, a distortion of speech and thus of the relationship between worshippers, and between them and God?

Despite the printed liturgical text, there are many places where worshippers are reminded of the exteriorized, oral and auditory nature of the activity. They are enjoined to 'listen to the holy gospel . . .'; to join with angels and archangels in singing the Sanctus; calls to repentance are not immediately met with lived examples of *metanoia*, but with the recitation of a text; the Eucharistic prayer repeats Christ's own words to the disciples; God's blessing on the congregation is conveyed through a written formula. It is not difficult for worshippers to imagine themselves in an oral context as the Bible, which is not only read in itself but is also the source and inspiration of most liturgical material,

---

[21]As Joyce Zimmerman has suggested, 'The text itself does not exhaust the meanings available to the worshipper in the worship event, it is not a "closed system of discourse" within the text', in idem., *Liturgy and Hermeneutics*, American Essays in Liturgy (Collegeville: The Liturgical Press, 1998), p. 69.

retains formal and linguistic structures which are characteristic of primary orality (as defined by Ong). Thus, we could cite the mnemonic nature of Genesis 1 or the Ten Commandments, the symmetrical account of the Last Supper in I Corinthians 11, the narrative and repetition of the psalter, etc. The purely oral is validated at many points throughout this text-based event.

Or we could reverse Ricoeur and suggest that liturgical worship is an event in which 'a discourse fixed by writing is spoken'. This, however, would reverse the customary relationship between speech and writing which is that speech precedes writing and that writing then replaces speech. Liturgical texts do certainly disrupt these conventions: the text does not preserve a prior spoken act, but is the means by which the speech can take place, and because it is performed, is it not imprisoned in a self-referential 'text world'. We could explore this historically, by charting the emergence of liturgical texts from the oral, improvisatory prayer of the earliest centuries,[22] or we could apply the same ideas to an examination of the process of producing new liturgical material in denominational committees.[23] In relation to contemporary liturgical creativity, we would need to consider whether indeed the written prayer text is related to any prior spoken prayer text at all, and the implications of a purely textual and literary approach to liturgical composition. Whereas in the earliest centuries the *libelli* were in effect an *aide-mémoire* for the bishop, and worship was conducted with recourse to patterns of words and themes woven together, but not written and recorded for reuse; historical and contemporary liturgical texts contain the liturgical event itself, all that is missing is the congregation and the situation in time and space. Liturgical books always contain the potential for worship, but in a different way than a group of Christians has within them the potential to worship. For people, the ideal is constant worship – both in explicit prayer and in

---

[22]See Allan Bouley, *From Freedom to Formula: The Evolution of the Eucharistic Prayer from Oral Improvisation to Written Texts* (Washington, DC: Catholic University of America Press, 1981).

[23]An awareness of these tensions is evident in a book of liturgical resources prepared by the Baptist Union of Great Britain which emphasizes the freedom characteristic of 'free church worship' while at the same time providing texts to serve as models for that worship. See Christopher J. Ellis and Myra Blyth (eds) for The Baptist Union of Great Britain, *Gathering for Worship. Patterns and Prayers for the Community of Disciples* (Norwich: Canterbury Press, 2005).

all aspects of life, the book requires worship in clearly demarcated parcels of time. This worship begins with 'Introductory Rites' and concludes with a 'Dismissal'; it is thus essentially time-bound and time-limited.

For much of our discussion in this and subsequent chapters, we will use 'text' to denote what Barthes calls the 'work'. However, if we were to shift our use of 'text' closer to his understanding of it as language, as signification, as the place where meaning is constructed between producer and reader/worshipper, then this might allow us to think about how the work functions in the liturgical event. To cite him in ways he would not have expected, 'the liturgical work is held in the hand, the text is the worship'. The text would be greater than the marks on the page, but would include all other signifiers in the worship event – rituals, dress, space, etc. His 'text' as object of study is then multifaceted and naturally this will be useful in our concluding discussion of the text (i.e. work) in performance; however, given the premiss of this book that it is the 'work' which dominates the liturgical event, but does so in unremarked ways that need much closer examination, we will return to our preferred use of 'text' in relation to the printed and written words of the liturgy.

We have suggested that the liturgical text is not the record of speech, although in composition it may have been spoken aloud, and is the recorded activity of revision committees; the text does not record the speech of a private prayer, as will be made very clear in later discussions about genre and intertextuality. But, then unlike a textbook which may have had its origins in spoken lectures and seminar discussions, the liturgical text does not replace speech. That is, it is not a means of preserving prior speech for an audience that was not present. So we find here the limitations of Saussure's definitions – the liturgical writing does not represent speech so much as facilitate it. It functions in completely the opposite way. What does exist before is what Ricouer calls 'discourse' – that which is intended to be communicated either by writing or speech. The liturgical text does contain a prior discourse which at some point in history was solely spoken, but is now almost always written; fixing the discourse in writing preserves it and that has created the conditions where normative forms of transmitting the discourse are established. The meaning, though, remains open to the interpretative strategies of the individual 'reader' and will be mediated communally through other signs (rituals) which have normative status.

Ong though reminds us that for literates the text intrudes upon meaning-making as we have so internalized the sign system of the script on the page that we are able to read without recourse to vocalization, such that writing functions as a visual sign. The liturgy is full of visual signs – gestures, movements, clothing, objects, etc. – and we might wish to add text to that list. Indeed, some Christians have accepted that liturgical texts act as visual signs by placing them on walls and above altars; many reformed churches replaced wall paintings of biblical and non-biblical scenes with texts of the Lord's Prayer, the Ten Commandments and the creed, for example.

The liturgy is not a remnant of primary orality and the words for prayer take on the same impersonality of all printed texts, or even more so than, say, a novel because of its anonymous authors (see Chapter 2). Ironically, a further demonstration of a move away from orality is in text which makes provision for improvisation. The *Directory of Public Worship* of 1644 which provided guidance on the conduct of worship to replace the banned Book of Common Prayer decries the idolatrous and unthinking recitation of the set words and urges the minister to exercise his ministry of prayer; however, probably wisely, it provides a fulsome resumé of what sort of words and themes are suitable.[24] Similarly in contemporary liturgical books, it is not uncommon for prayers and introductory addresses to be preceded by the rubric, 'The minister says these or other suitable words'. In my experience, the minister very rarely exercises the option. Daniel E. Albrecht in his analysis of Pentecostal/charismatic worship has also remarked on the fixity of words even if these are not necessarily inscribed in an authoritative text.[25] These examples indicate how far from primary orality our liturgy is.

There is a paradox evident in the assertions by, say, Derrida or Ong about the impermanence of speech in relation to the permanence of writing and theological ideas about the permanence of worship. Christians are enjoined to 'pray without ceasing' (1 Thessalonians 5.17) and the worship on earth joins with and prefigures the never-ending worship around the throne of God, so by its nature it is not impermanent. What is permanent here is

---

[24]See *The Directory for Public Worship*, 1644 (authorized in 1645 in Scotland). Text available at <http://www.epcew.org.uk/dpw/> [accessed 27 March 2012].
[25]Daniel E. Albrect, *Rites in the Spirit: A Ritual Approach to Pentecostal/Charismatic Spirituality* (Sheffield: Sheffield Academic Press, 1999).

clearly not a text which endures long after the liturgical event and its speech have disappeared, but rather a discourse of praise. Sara Irwin has suggested that liturgy forms its own third genre between speech and writing:

> [Liturgical] speech that is spoken is tied not to the speaker, but to the community, to those who went before and those who will come after. Speech that is spoken liturgically 'belongs' to no one, is directed to God; the assembled body speaks, in a sense, but is also spoken as they open themselves to God's purpose. Neither the permanence of writing nor the ephemeral nature of speech can account for how things are done with words and bodies in the liturgy.[26]

Whether the liturgy is any more of a third genre than a play is debatable; in this article, she pays considerably less attention to the liturgical text than to the liturgical speech.

Despite the liturgy's origins in orality, the liturgical text has moved further and further away even from a sort of secondary orality based on memorizing the texts to be used. One of Cranmer's justifications for producing a single book to replace the regional rites was that reading an unfamiliar book would be profitable:

> And where heretofore, there hath been great diversitie in saying and synging in churches within this realme: . . . Now from hencefurth, all the whole realme shall have but one use. And if any would judge this waye more painfull, because that all thynges must be read upon the boke, whereas before, by the reason of so often repeticion, they could saye many thinges by heart: if those men will waye their labor, with the profite in knowlege, whiche dayely they shal obtein by readyng upon the boke, they will not refuse the payn, in consideracion of the greate profite that shall ensue therof.[27]

Liturgical reform based on producing a new liturgical text has been very commonplace in recent decades. It is interesting to note

---

[26]Sara H. Irwin, 'The Religiophenome: Liturgy and Some Uses of Deconstruction', *Worship* 80 (2006), p. 243.

[27]Thomas Cranmer, Preface to the BCP, 1549. <http://justus.anglican.org/resources/bcp/1549/front_matter_1549.htm#Preface> [accessed 29 July 2013].

that the principal response to worship which appears out-dated is to produce a new text to replace the old one and not revitalize the old, either by modernizing the language or reviving the ritual. Since the middle of the twentieth century, liturgical revision has been almost exclusively considered as a textual matter; the revision committees put out new text, and even furnish it with explanatory notes or a commentary; the parishes use the new text in worship and if it does not 'work' they complain on the basis that the text is too long and/or too complicated. These two complaints reveal a very interesting attitude to producing the new text; on the one hand, often the liturgical event has been lengthened by the addition of new ritual and textual elements, but conversely the prayer texts themselves have been cut to the barest minimum with the aim of simplification. The consequence of the cutting is to remove the sort of repetitive and elaborative features which orality requires and thus, in a self-defeating cycle, the literariness of the text becomes extremely prominent. Following Ong's distinctions, a concise and refined text produced in a literate context is suited to private reading and often requires rereading to be fully appreciated, and so it is not surprising it does not 'work' in a liturgical event where the text is completed before even a preliminary grasp of its content or meaning is possible.

Readers, speakers and worshippers

It would be naïve to suggest that participants are able to suspend their normal relationship to texts in the context of an act of worship when printed matter is thrust into their hands at the door and competent participation is dependent upon locating and using the texts to which they are directed during the course of that worship. So the second issue which arises is what is the relationship between reader and text, between worshipper and text, and how do these relationships differ from that between two participants in a dialogue.

Ong remarks on the exteriority of sight and the interiority of sound: sound comes to us and is internalized; sight goes out from us and that which we see or read always exists externally. Speech also comes from within us and goes into the other people who hear it, and so 'it manifests human beings to one another as conscious interiors, as persons'.[28] Pertinently for our discussion of liturgical worship, he remarks

> When a speaker is addressing an audience, the members of the audience normally become a unity, with themselves and with the speaker. If the speaker asks the audience to read a handout provided for them, as each reader enters into his or her own private reading world, the unity of the audience is shattered, to be re-established only when oral speech begins again. Writing and print isolate.[29]

This is something that can be often witnessed in churches where a procession to the centre of the nave to read the gospel ritualizes Christ speaking in the midst of his people, but the people are not listening but reading the text of that gospel provided in that Sunday's service leaflet. Externally and ritually, speech has been prioritized, but internally, and by an alternative ritual, text provided to be helpful has intruded and become a barrier to the listener receiving the speech. What they interiorize is a text read privately, as with almost all other texts they might read. When worshippers become readers, the context does not make them a different kind of reader, and they will bring to this context all the reading strategies they use in other aspects of their life, both to undertake the task of reading itself and in the process of discerning meaning.

Worshippers are also speakers, but their speech is controlled by the texts; nevertheless providers of these texts and the users share an understanding that the texts contain legitimate and appropriate speech to and about God to which the faithful should or may not object. Irwin has noted how the speech of the assembly 'belongs to no one' and that it is the assembly as a whole which speaks.[30] Yes, but this is to ignore the different conversation-type activities which occur throughout (dialogues, litanies, etc.). Frequent repetition of certain texts may cause them to be memorized after which they can take on a new life free from the printed text, but that does

---

[28]Ong, *Orality and Literacy*, p. 73.
[29]Ibid.
[30]Irwin, 'Religiophenome', p. 243.

not accord them the status of primary orality. Following Ong, if speech exteriorizes and reading interiorizes, then the worshipper and the assembly have to navigate between the two in order to find an appropriate level of participation which balances the individual and the communal. Denominations with set forms of liturgy have traditionally asserted the communal over individual, whereas those with free worship have emphasized individual participation; these distinctions break down though when literacy displaces orality in the worship event.

Some functions of the liturgical text

The text we use does serve other purposes than simply facilitating a religious encounter. I have discussed above how possession of the text is related to power in the community, this continues in the liturgy by certain texts being reserved for particular people – these may be distinguished by their place in the hierarchy or by gender, or occasionally age. Thus the performance of the text has 'authority' embedded in it in each particular act of worship, as well as the book itself being authoritative. Churches with set forms of liturgy place great store by the rules which govern the exclusive use of their liturgical texts; extracts from civil law or canon law may be included in the printed books to make that extremely clear, or the authorization of the text carries the force of law. In previous centuries, deviations from the text by omissions and interpolations would have been met by legal processes, such as those against ritualists in England in the nineteenth century or dissenters in the seventeenth. Such authority is de-personalized despite the liturgical text extending the reach of the churches' authority structures into each and every congregation which submits to the book.

Related to this is the question of identity. The rituals and words of worship form the worshippers as the people of God, they shape attitudes to each other, to God and to the world; they enable a transformation or reformation of identity as one's own narrative is inserted into the narrative of salvation; they make present the kingdom of God.[31] So just as individual identity is formed through

---

[31]See Chapter 5.

the liturgical texts used, so too is the community as a whole. The use of a particular liturgical text, or even none at all, serves to distinguish different ecclesial groups, and in the recent past allegiance to certain historic texts has led to the creation of organizations to promote the use of such a text, for example the Latin Mass Society or the Prayer Book Society. For their members, these historic texts preserve the essence of their denomination's identity, in a way that contemporary texts are perceived not to; it has to be noted that modern texts do not have such supporters clubs. These historic texts are promoted as authentic expressions of the denomination's beliefs and practices.

The principal churches with set and authorized liturgical forms are large national and pan-national organizations and the use of the same liturgical text throughout its local churches is both a sign and instrument of unity. This has been understood at both an official and a popular level: two examples will suffice. When Elizabeth I restored the Book of Common Prayer in 1559, appended to the front of the Book was a reissued Parliamentary 'Act of Uniformity' which insisted that only this book was to be used by ministers, that the people were to take themselves to church on Sundays, by implication to pray using this book, and the Act detailed the penalties for not doing so. From recent years, the translation principles articulated by the Roman Catholic Church establish norms to ensure that the text used at Mass in different language groups is directly comparable to the *editio typica*; that is, it is the text which ensures unity of worship, and thus fosters and demonstrates the unity of the Church.

Conclusion

Liturgical studies which concentrate on textual interpretation will often look at the meaning of the text: what does it say, what is its theology, what are its sources? In this book we shall concentrate on the specifically textual aspects of the liturgical text, that is not what it says but how it says it. Readers ask 'who wrote this book?' and seek to contextualize the content by identifying the author; they ask 'what type of book is this?' and from that know what it is likely to contain and for what purpose; they look for consecutive units of meaning, the narrative; they become aware that the text makes reference to other texts they know; they use linguistic units which are familiar and unfamiliar, everyday and yet not quite the language of everyday; and lastly their experience as book readers enables them to use the technology of the liturgical book. In the worship event, all these skills are deployed unconsciously by literate worshippers, and even those less literate will know that these skills are required when they fall short, that is when they cannot find their place on the page, and thus literacy skills affect participation.

2

Authorship[1]

In the previous chapter, I explored the nature of the liturgical text in relation to its historical development and in light of contemporary philosophical and literary studies. It was Ricouer who reminded us that a text is the product of an activity in addition to a physical item; here we turn our attention to the process of producing liturgical texts, and specifically to ideas around authorship. What we shall note is the overwhelming importance of the author in relation to historical texts and the near absence of interest where contemporary liturgical texts are concerned. The reluctance by contemporary worshippers to look for an author may well stem from their desire to 'own' for themselves the words they speak in the liturgy, but nevertheless these texts have been produced and it is usually considered by human efforts. In the following discussion, we shall note the difficulties to find a definition of what it might be to 'author' these texts using notions of authorship drawn from literature or scientific writing, and we will discover that liturgical authorship involves a more diffused process of production. Finally, to help us towards this book's investigation of the role of the text in the worship event, we shall ask what function the 'author' serves for worshippers.

The author is dead!

It is a paradox in liturgical studies that any scholarly examination of an historical text will usually begin with an investigation into the life, career and works of the author to whom it is attributed,

---

[1]This chapter is a revision of my 'Liturgical Authorship', published in *Anaphora* 3, no. 2 (2009), pp. 39–56.

whereas studies of contemporary liturgical material are never concerned with the question of who wrote the text. Why is it that an historical text can only properly reveal its meaning through an examination of its composition in a specific time and place by a specific individual, whereas a contemporary text, it is assumed, needs no such contextualization in relation to an author? The latter is all the more curious given the discussion in churches with authorized liturgical texts about the inculturation of the liturgy, a further paradox is revealed in that the culture of a text's origin is not in question so much as the culture where it is to be used. Roland Barthes proclaimed the author to be dead;[2] the historical liturgical author certainly is, but can we say the same for the contemporary liturgical author?

Behind Barthes's provocative declaration of the author's death was a desire to liberate the reader from the oppressive situation where meaning could only be determined in relation to what the author intended to convey; he concluded that 'the birth of the reader must be at the cost of the author'.[3] And Michel Foucault, asking 'What is an author?',[4] expressed how the privileging of the author 'allows a limitation of the cancerous and dangerous proliferation of signification'; the author is 'the principle of thrift in the proliferation of meaning'.[5] Because once we have identified an author we need to take their intentions into account in our interpretation of the text, the text ceases to have a life of its own in the world and we are restricted in the meanings we can generate from it. As we shall explore later on, authorship is related to the interpretation of texts, as well as their production; to what extent are we dependent upon the author for our appropriation of a liturgical text's meaning?

The missing author from contemporary texts may relate to Martin Stringer's statement that there are as many meanings of a liturgical performance as there are participants and by implication, contemporary liturgical texts have a life independent of the author:

---

[2]Roland Barthes, 'The Death of the Author' [first published in French in 1968], idem., *Image, Music, Text*, pp. 142–8.
[3]Ibid., p. 148.
[4]Michel Foucault, 'What is an Author?' [first published in French in 1969], in Josué Harari (ed.), *Textual Strategies: Perspectives in Post-structural Criticism* (London: Methuen, 1979), pp. 141–60.
[5]Ibid., p. 159.

is Barthes's statement therefore true?[6] Or, we might want to go with Foucault's restriction of the 'author-function' to specific types of texts;[7] might we wish to say that liturgical texts, like letters or laundry lists, are authorless? If we did, we would seriously hamper the aim of historical liturgical studies which is to provide a coherent narrative of the development of Christian worship which necessarily requires attentiveness to the context of composition. It would seem to be illogical to assert that the contemporary text is authorless while the historical text is authored as, regardless of when they were composed, liturgical texts display some quite strong family resemblances.[8] Any examination of liturgical authorship, then, needs to begin with the type of texts we are dealing with, which reflects the manner in which liturgical texts are produced and how they are interpreted.

The presence or absence of an author is directly connected with the issue of what a text means. Every time a critical edition discusses the attribution of a text, it does so on the premise that it is possible to identify a named person who is responsible for the creation of that liturgical text and, once correctly attributed, our knowledge of the author will assist us in interpreting it.[9] Contemporary liturgical studies concern themselves almost exclusively with the issue of interpretation in light of the theological presuppositions of the commentator, of the performance of the liturgy in the congregation, and of the effectiveness of the transfer of meaning from minister to worshippers. The revision process by church authorities may be described, as in, for example, Bugnini's *Reform of the Liturgy* and David Hebblethwaite's *Liturgical Revision in the Church of England*,[10] without identifying individual contributions and the text

---

[6]Martin Stringer, *On the Perception of Worship* (Birmingham: University of Birmingham Press, 1999), p. 2 and elsewhere.

[7]Foucault, 'What is an Author?', p. 148.

[8]See Chapter 3 for the stability of liturgical genres.

[9]See, for example, discussions about whether Basil of Caesarea composed the Anaphora or even the Liturgy of St Basil in John F. Fenwick, *The Anaphoras of St Basil and St James. An Investigation into their Common Origin*, OCA 240 (Rome: Pontificium Institutum Studiorum Orientalium, 1992), pp. 19–22, and the numerous different attributions of the Roman Canon discussed in my 'Interpreting the Origins of the Roman Canon', *Studia Patristica* 71 (2013), pp. 53–67.

[10]Annibale Bugnini, *The Reform of the Liturgy 1948–1975* (Collegeville: Liturgical Press, 1990); David Hebblethwaite, *Liturgical Revision in the Church of England, 1984–2004*, Alcuin/GROW Liturgical Study 57 (Cambridge: Grove Books, 2004).

is always used and interpreted independently of an author.[11] This is curious given that most liturgical texts correspond to certain genres with, arguably, predetermined intentions. So, an author's intention when writing a Eucharistic prayer is to provide an appropriate means of consecrating the Eucharistic elements; that intention remains the same regardless of whether the prayer was composed in the fourth century or the twentieth century. Consequently, it would seem legitimate to look for a model of authorship which would hold true for any type of liturgical text in any age, which holds true for our understanding of text production as well as interpretation.

The popular notion of authorship asserts that an author is the single unified creative origin of a written work, the producer of a text. This sort of author became possible once he/she could be identified after the onset of printing and copyright laws and following the Romantics' reflection on the process of literary creativity. Attribution studies in literature and liturgy rely upon such a notion even if it is not explicitly acknowledged. As we have said, it would be rare to find a critical edition or study of an historical liturgical text which did not begin with an investigation into its authorship, where the text is related to the attributed author's other writings and their socio-historical context; or, conversely, where the attribution is disputed on the basis of inconsistencies between the liturgical text and other texts or the presumed context. The level of originality required by a liturgical author would appear to be much less than that expected of a literary author and we easily note that many liturgical texts share structural and linguistic features even when no direct connection between them can be demonstrated; examples from the fourth century might include the convergence in the formula for renouncing the devil in baptismal liturgies and the structure of anaphoras.[12]

---

[11]Identification of the author and translator is expressly forbidden in the Roman Catholic Church with the implied reason that the liturgical books are the work of the whole church, see *Liturgicae Instaurationes* (Instruction on the orderly carrying out of the Constitution on the Liturgy, September 5, 1970). The same document decries improvisation 'which can only trivialize the liturgy'. <http://www.ewtn.com/library/CURIA/CDWLITUR.HTM> [accessed 12 August 2013].

[12]For the former see, for example, the discussion in chapter 4 of my *The Baptismal Liturgy of Jerusalem: Fourth and Fifth Century Evidence from Palestine, Syria, and Egypt* (Aldershot: Ashgate Publishing, 2007). For the latter, a cursory read through the collected eucharistic prayers in a compendium such as Anton Hänggi and Irmgard Pahl, *Prex eucharistica. Volumen I: Textus e variis liturgiis antiqui-oribus selecti* (Fribourg: Éditions Universitaires, 1968), or for English translations,

Authors of historical liturgical texts: Serapion and his sacramentary

The debate over the authorship of the collection of prayers attributed to Serapion is a useful example with which to highlight some of these issues; particularly as the text is relatively short and the discussion therefore confined. Serapion was bishop of Thmuis in Egypt in the early/mid-fourth century, and was a correspondent of both the 'founder of monasticism', Anthony of Egypt, and the arch-Nicene, Athanasius. Already we become aware that this biographical information anticipates a certain context, spirituality and theology for the prayers. If we are lucky enough to have other texts which are attributed to our liturgical author, then these too can be used to interpret the liturgical text, and in many cases this is done regardless of the different production processes and intentions for the non-liturgical material. We have to ask, though, whether knowing other texts assists primarily the attribution or the interpretation. In relation to Serapion's text, Maxwell Johnson asserted that, 'The accuracy of a liturgical document's attribution to a specific author can only be based upon a number of parallels between the liturgical text and other authentic works of that author.'[13] Of course this is a pragmatic way of checking attributions, but it inevitably risks a somewhat circular process whereby on the basis of a name appearing in a manuscript, a context and a relationship to other texts bearing the same name are presumed; that context and the other texts then serve to confirm the initial attribution. Context too can be misleading or at least produce quite different attributions: Geoffrey Cuming assigned the final form of the sacramentary to Serapion 'bishop of Thmuis, friend of Athanasius' on the basis of the context implied by its theological content,[14] whereas Bernard Botte was so unconvinced by the Nicene orthodoxy

---

R. C. D. Jasper and G. J. Cuming, *Prayers of the Eucharist: Early and Reformed* (3rd ed. Collegeville: Liturgical Press, 1990).

[13]Maxwell E. Johnson, *The Prayers of Sarapion of Thmuis: A Literary, Liturgical and Theological Analysis.* OCA 259 (Rome: Pontificium Institutum Studiorum Orientalium, 1995), p. 282.

[14]G. J. Cuming, 'Thmuis Revisited: Another Look at the Prayers of Bishop Sarapion', *TS* 41 (1980), p. 575.

of the sacramentary that he placed it in an Arian context from the end of the century![15] What is important here is the role of context in relation to the production and interpretation of historical liturgical texts; it is accepted that the author is affected by intellectual and social factors and, by implication, that in the historic worship event the text was perfectly suited to the situation and culture of the people of Thmuis.

The most obvious way of identifying an author is to look for his or her name in the text and so the presence of Serapion's name twice in the manuscript at the head of two prayers (prayer 1, the anaphora; prayer 15, the first oil prayer) should be conclusive. But what exactly does this attribution indicate? F. E. Brightman concluded on the basis of these names that the whole collection should be attributed to Serapion because 'it is not uncommon in liturgical documents to find the real or supposed author's name attached to the titles of individual prayers of a series, the whole of which is meant to be attributed to the same author'.[16] Of course, the whole collection could be attributed to Serapion by the additional evidence provided by structural and stylistic factors; if all the prayers share the same characteristics then, as Bernard Capelle, we might wish to identify '[le] génie novateur de l'évêque Sérapion'.[17] Or, one might take a more conservative approach and only assert that Serapion was the author of the prayers to which his name is attached, again using the same criteria of structure and style.[18] To this we would observe that the attribution is not contained in the prayers but in words which surround the prayer (what Gérard Genette calls the 'paratext'[19]), in much the same way as the title page of a novel gives us the name of the acknowledged author even though the text itself may be unable to reveal the identity of that author.[20] We commonly denote

---

[15]Bernard Botte, 'L'Eucologe de Sérapion est-il authentique?', *OrChr* 48 (1964), pp. 50–6.

[16]F. E. Brightman, 'The Sacramentary of Serapion', *JTS* 1 (1900), p. 90.

[17]Bernard Capelle, 'L'Anaphore de Sérapion. Essai d'Exégèse', *Le Muséon* 59 (1946), p. 443.

[18]P. Drews, 'Über Wobbermins "Altchristliche liturgische Stücke aus der Kirche Aegyptens"', *ZKG* 20 (1900), pp. 291–328 and 415–41.

[19]Gérard Genette, *Paratexts: Thresholds of Interpretation* (Cambridge: Cambridge University Press, 1997). See Chapter 7 for a discussion of this in relation to liturgical texts.

[20]Botte ('L'Eucologe de Sérapion', p. 51) also questioned whether the presence of Serapion's name was sufficient evidence for the attribution of authorship.

as the author the one whose name appears in the text but this may
not be as conclusive as it appears and it may raise a whole range
of other problems. Readers of literature appear happy to read a
book published under a *nom-de-plûme* and even fill in contextual
details for that rather than the 'real' author; an example might be
the original readers of the nineteenth-century English writer Mary
Ann Evans who believed that they were reading the works of the
male author George Elliot. The presence of a name on a text then
serves only a limited function: from it we may infer a context of
composition which may offer some assistance to interpretation,
but that too can be misleading. What it completely fails to reveal,
though, is the process of production and the multiple influences
upon the text's creation.

Where a text displays evidence of revision, discussion revolves
around the point in the text's production at which the named author
is supposed to have exerted the dominant and defining influence.
These texts can reveal the editorial process when there is clear
evidence of borrowing from another source which is embedded in
a recognizable way in the text. In such instances the named author
is no longer an innovative genius and his role is now perceived to
carry much less status; he is merely an editor. The overt reference to
Didache 9.4 in the anaphora to which, we must remember, Serapion's
name is attached, led Wobbermin to conclude that Serapion was
just the final redactor of the text.[21] Cuming, too, determined that
the sacramentary was made up of various collections of prayers
which displayed the work of several hands, Serapion's role being
that of the final editor.[22] And Johnson concurred, noting that the
prayers available for the compilation already displayed different
historical strata and expressing uncertainty whether indeed
Serapion had anything to do with the document.[23] The text itself
reveals the multiple layers independently of the named author which
casts doubt on the reliability of the attribution, although all three
scholars might continue to talk about the Sacramentary of Serapion
rather than the Sacramentary of Thmuis because of the strength of

[21]G. Wobbermin, *Altchristliche liturgische Stücke aus der Kirche Aegyptus nebst einem dogmatischen Brief des Bischofs Serapion von Thmuis*, TU 18 (Leipzig and Berlin: J. C. Hinrichs, 1898), p. 31.
[22]Cuming, 'Thmuis Revisited', pp. 572, 575.
[23]Johnson, *Prayers of Sarapion*, p. 281.

tradition. It may not be appropriate then, to consider Serapion as the creative originator of the text but (only) as an editor.

Attributing authorship

As we have seen, trying to identify what sort of 'author' Serapion was elicits some quite different responses, which begs the question as to why the sacramentary was attributed to him in the first place. Attribution studies is an established subdiscipline of literary studies but even though liturgical scholars have evaluated the reasons for attributing specific texts, few have enquired into the manner in which it occurs. The exceptions are the brief essays concerning the *Liturgy of St John Chrysostom*, and particularly its anaphora, by Geoffrey Cuming and Robert Taft.

Cuming identified three categories of attribution.[24]

1   Liturgies attributed to an apostle or other notable figure where the name is chosen to give authority to the text but none would consider them responsible for it: 'pseudonymous attribution'.

2   Liturgies attributed to a notable figure where the attribution is 'in all probability correct', even though positive evidence may be lacking: 'authentic attribution'.

3   And between these categories, attributions which may be pseudonymous or authentic. The named author may be sufficiently well known to attract attention to the text bearing his name (hence the risk of pseudonymity), but he flourished at the right time for the attribution (hence the possibility of authenticity).

The particular issue with the *Liturgy of Chrysostom* concerns whether simply the anaphora is to be attributed to him, or the whole liturgy, or parts of the whole. Cuming provides three criteria for establishing the attribution of an anaphora:

---

[24]G. J. Cuming, 'Pseudonymity and Authenticity, with Special Reference to the Liturgy of St John Chrysostom', *Studia Patristica* 15 (1984), p. 532.

1   The presence in other writings by the proposed author of
    words or phrases which appear in the liturgical text, but, in
    the case of Chrysostom, noting his predilection for quoting
    liturgical texts in his homilies, Cuming said that an unusual
    phrase 'may be in the anaphora because it was a favourite
    phrase . . . or a favourite phrase because it was in the
    anaphora'.[25]

2   The use in the prayer and in authentic writings of phrases
    that were 'in the air', stock phrases, *formelgut*. An
    investigation into this will concern what is meant by the
    composition of prayers in the ancient church, to what extent
    was the bishop free to compose an original text and the
    extent to which he was constrained by expectations and
    conventions about structure and substance.

3   Stylistic analysis offers a more subjective judgement than
    the previous two: does the prayer feel like something
    Chrysostom might have written on the basis of his other
    writings? Since Cuming wrote this the use of computer
    stylistic analysis has been used by a number of scholars to
    indicate stylistic parallels in texts with disputed attributions
    and Taft has welcomed the speed with which this task can
    now be accomplished.[26]

Cuming's analysis is useful for our purpose in that he notes how
very fluid the notion of authorship is, but what underlies it is an
assumption that, given a complete set of data, an individual creative
figure can be identified, even if he is not the person named at the
head of the text.

Categorizing authorship as pseudonymous, authentic and
somewhere-in-between helps us to distinguish how the named
author relates to the text and permits assumptions about his role
in producing the text; admittedly these assumptions may only
be accurate in relation to the first category! Cuming highlights,
in relation to historical liturgical texts, what Foucault called the
'author-function' and how we unconsciously appeal to an author

---

[25]Ibid., p. 535.
[26]Robert F. Taft, 'The Authenticity of the Chrysostom Anaphora Revisited.
Determining the Authorship of Liturgical Texts by Computer', *OCP* 56 (1990),
p. 22.

when validating our interpretations. Only if a text is known to be pseudonymous will we exercise caution when interpreting it in relation to other texts by the person whose name is used, but what is it about the content and implied context which has caused the erroneous attribution in the first place? Cuming's counterpart to pseudonymity is authenticity, by which he means that the attribution is correct rather than any value judgement on the nature of the text itself, as even erroneously attributed texts have been authored and are just as likely to have been used in a liturgical context. To say that John Chrysostom did not compose the *Liturgy of St John Chrysostom* does not invalidate the text as a liturgical text: it is not the same as saying that the *Hitler Diaries* are a forgery.

The work on Serapion and John Chrysostom clarify for us some of the problems in identifying anyone as an author in the sense of original creative genius. These liturgical texts demonstrate that the authors have been subject to tradition which predates them such that they have incorporated stock phrases and structures; the texts which bear their name have been subject to editorial processes; that the named authors may stand at the start of this editing or the end; that 'compiler' may be a better designation than 'author', and that the relationship between the written text or earliest stratum and the improvisatory liturgical tradition remains unresolved. What is required is a model of authorship applicable to historical and contemporary liturgical texts which allows for text production in conditions of limited creative freedom, involving more than one person, and for this we might turn to theories of authorship arising from literary studies.

Collaborative authorship and creativity

Harold Love provides a useful model. He conceived of authorship as a collaborative process, 'a series of functions performed during the creation of a work rather than a single coherent activity',[27] and identified four 'linked activities':[28]

---

[27]Harold Love, *Attributing Authorship* (Cambridge: Cambridge University Press, 2002), p. 39.
[28]Ibid., pp. 40–9.

- Precursory authorship where a significant amount of material has been taken from previously existing sources, either by influence or direct borrowing.

- Executive authorship which closely resembles the traditional notion of 'author'; she is the one who devises, orders, compiles and makes a text ready for publication. This may be achieved by more than one person, although the sole executor carries greater esteem.

- Declarative authorship consists of the process of a text's validation by a named individual whose involvement in its production may be severely limited or non-existent, but who nevertheless influences the contextualization and interpretation of the text. Love includes here the retrospective attribution of authorship to an anonymous text, as well as ghost-writing.

- Revisionary authorship occurs after the creation of a text when it may be polished or corrected, edited or revised by a second author or editor.

If we return to our discussion of the authorship and attribution criteria for the sacramentary of Serapion, we will notice that the different conclusions about the production of the final text have placed Serapion in each of these four categories. Where it has been concluded that he has drawn upon previously existing material and simply collected it together, he is a revisionary author; where he has been considered the composer of the text, he is the executive author. If, though, we decide that he is not responsible for the final text but that there is evidence of later redactions, then might he be considered the precursory author? Or, if the attribution is entirely erroneous, is he simply the declarative author? Love's schema will not solve the question of the authorship of the sacramentary, but by prioritizing collaboration over individual creativity it provides a theory of authorship which more closely fits the varied evidence which this and other texts present.

Love's framework also seems to fit our notions of authorship in relation to the production of contemporary liturgical texts such as the Church of England's *Common Worship*, an example of anonymous and collaborative authorship. The production of the text was charged to a Liturgical Commission whose corporate role in the authorship of the texts was diffused; much of the composition and editing happened in subcommittees who themselves were influenced by correspondence and reports of experimental use of the liturgies. Although there are new liturgical compositions, many existing texts were retained or edited, and other older traditional texts were (re-)introduced. Thus the final text presents a mixture of precursory, executive and revisionary authorship and the Liturgical Commission might be designated as the declarative author, even though the copyright asserts ownership by the 'ARCHBISHOPS' COUNCIL/CHURCH OF ENGLAND'. It would be impossible for any but those actually present in the subcommittees to attribute sole creative authorship to any one of their members, and even original compositions would have been subject to amendment and revision during the process. What can be said about *Common Worship* also holds true for all recently authorized liturgical texts in the Western churches where text production is in the hands of a committee and collaboration is the norm. The reluctance to speak about 'authorship' in relation to these contemporary texts may well be based on the assumption that an author can only be the lone creative genius. Collaborative authorship may provide us with the terminology to talk about the origin, production and authority of contemporary texts, although it says little about the role of the author in textual interpretation.

F. E. Brightman, noted that, 'The greater part of any fully developed liturgy is likely to be common form, and marks of individual authorship are only to be looked for in occasional features, whether dogmatic statement or of characteristic or favourite phraseology. . . .'[29] We have noted the dependence upon stock phrases in liturgical texts, which is evident even in relatively early texts. The use of such phrases may well arise from the author's intention to produce a text with a recognizable genre which conforms to the expectations of the recipients of the text, and is determined by traditions in that community and by theological preferences. Structurally, and verbally in places, Serapion's anaphora is not dissimilar to other fourth-century Eucharistic prayers, although the striking presence of an epiclesis of the *Logos*, and not of the Holy Spirit, marks off for us a clear innovation driven by the author's theological intentions. Contemporary Eucharistic prayers,

---

[29]F. E. Brightman, 'The Anaphora of Theodore', *JTS* 3 (1930), p. 161.

too, rarely do anything radical with the structure or language; most simply adapt existing patterns. There are limits, then, to the ability of the text's producer to function as an original creative genius even in the halcyon days when the bishop was at liberty to improvise. Allan Bouley charted the move from Eucharistic prayers which, in the pre-Nicene church, were 'freely improvised', even though conventions restricted the creativity of the minister, to the appearance of and dependence upon written texts which became increasingly fixed and literary.[30] This very valuable study provides the evidence from which we can chart the increasing convergence and rigidity of prayers but it does not give any insights into the production methods of improvised or written texts; for this liturgists might usefully look at studies into the mechanism of creating oral poetry in non-literate cultures and the effect of writing upon that process. The relationship between orality and text has long been a feature of Homeric studies and saga studies, but not liturgical studies, and useful insights can I think be gleaned from the work of Albert Lord in 1930s Yugoslavia among the illiterate singers of traditional tales.[31]

Lord noted that oral epic songs are not renditions of previously existing memorized or written text, but that they are created during the performance and thus each song is a new composition, even though the singer and audience will be familiar with its contents. The illiterate singers built up songs using formulaic expressions and themes. Lord defined 'formula' as a group of words regularly used to express a given essential idea in the same metrical conditions, by 'theme' he understood the repeated incidents, descriptive passages or the grouping of ideas.[32] Both formulae and themes are not restricted to specific songs, 'stories', but are adopted and adapted as need arises during the performance. Thus, Lord says,

> When the singer of tales, equipped with a store of formulas and themes and a technique of composition, takes his place before an audience and tells his story, he follows the plan which he has learned along with the other elements of his profession. Whereas

---

[30]Bouley, *Freedom to Formula*, p. 89, see pp. 89–158.
[31]Albert B. Lord, *The Singer of Tales*, 2nd ed. revised by S. Mitchell and G. Nagy (Cambridge, MA: Harvard University Press, 2001). The first edition was published in 1960.
[32]Ibid., p. 4.

the singer thinks of his song as a flexible pattern of themes, some
of which are essential and some of which are not, we think of it
as a given text which undergoes change from one singing to the
next. . . .[33]

For the singer, the stability of the story does not reside in the
words, but in the narrative. In such a technique there is not an
original text from which a performer deviates, nor is there a point
of origin; the 'author' of the song is the performer at the moment
of performance, but he is dependent upon all the other singers he
has heard performing this same song. Thus 'authorship' in such
a production method is ephemeral and diffuse. What happens
when a performance is recorded is to capture the tradition at that
particular point, but our relationship to written texts leads us to
presume that what we have recorded is an authoritative version of
that song.[34] Such written versions are not transitional between oral
and written culture but the capturing of a single performance which
has little immediate effect upon the oral tradition, which continues
regardless by the illiterate singers. Lord did note that the circulation
of written songs, either composed from a number of performances
of the same story or the record of a single performance, caused the
singer's role to change into one of memorizing and repeating, and it
introduced the possibility of incorrect recitation: a move from 'the
stability of the essential story which is the goal of the oral tradition,
to the stability of the text, the exact words of the story'.[35]
    Here we have the opportunity to investigate a fresh perspective
upon the manner in which liturgical texts may be authored. Unlike
Lord for these songs, we were not present at the moment of recording
the improvised prayer, but we can see traces of the use of themes
and formulae in the similarities and differences exhibited by early
anaphoras. What does it mean to be the author of a liturgical text in
an oral culture? Well, following Lord, it would be to create a prayer
at each liturgical event, the content of which would be determined
by the patterns available to the one praying, the expectations of
the worshippers who have been formed in the same tradition, the
linguistic skills of the priest in the appropriate expression of the

---

[33]Ibid., p. 99.
[34]Ibid., p. 125.
[35]Ibid., p. 138.

'themes' and 'formulas'. He will not be the author of a single text, but an author every time he prays. When he writes the prayer down, or it is recorded, he will not cease to draw upon the traditions, but will adopt a literary technique, such as one finds in the theological and literary refinement of developed prayers like that attributed to St James. Authorship in relation to texts which are based on a preceding oral tradition can only be envisaged as multiple, there cannot be a single creative origin, but instead a creative use of the traditions of structure and language in relation to the specific worshipping context.

Authority and meaning

We have mentioned already how the notion of authorship is related to interpreting the meaning of a text as well as the process of production and it is this that we shall now explore more systematically. There are, in principle, three basic approaches to this issue which assign different roles to the author. First, we could say that the meaning of the text is what the author intends; secondly, that the meaning of the text resides entirely in the text itself which is a self-contained entity; or thirdly, that meaning production is a collaboration between intention and interpretation.

The traditional notion of authorship presumed that an original creative genius wrote fully conscious of what he intended to convey and that the meaning of the text lay in revealing those intentions. This explains the emphasis upon identifying the author in literary and liturgical studies so as to use all available information about that author to produce an 'authoritative' interpretation. Even if we understand 'author' in the widest sense as a series of collaborative endeavours, as Love, then we can see that even contemporary liturgical texts are not immune from such a perception. Although the *Roman Missal* has no names attached, it is prefaced by the 'General Instruction' which provides a comprehensive theological and ritual interpretation of the liturgical text itself. General instructions attached to Roman Catholic liturgical texts are issued with the same authority as the liturgical text itself, and thus offer an authoritative interpretation not simply a secondary opinion.

With historical liturgical texts, we clearly have a problem
knowing the author's intention and here William Irwin's suggestion
of a separation of author figures might be useful. He distinguished
between 'an actual historical agent who produces a text and . . . a
figure we construct in interpreting that text'.[36] This second figure he
calls the 'author construct' or 'urauthor' which will 'be composed
of relevant available biographical information, likely intention, use
of language in the text itself, information concerning the author's
context and audience, and other texts of the author inasmuch as
they inform the other elements of the urauthor'.[37] Irwin claims that
such a figure can be discerned in every text; although the urauthor
is grounded in an historical person, the interpretation of the text
is not dependent on this figure but upon the figure we construct
in our thoughts to aid us in the interpretation of the text. The
urauthor can be given the name Serapion, but our construction of
him may well not be the same as an historical Serapion whom, in
any case, we cannot recover. The historical Serapion cannot control
the interpretations we place upon the prayers which bear his name,
but starting with whatever (historical) information we can gather
from within and without the text, we are then free to interpret:
'Interpretation must first involve historical understanding and only
later creativity,' says Irwin.[38]

The 'author construct' may also have its uses in relation to
contemporary texts. *Common Worship* appeared in a particular
social, linguistic, ecclesial and historical context. We are likely
to make grave errors in interpreting these texts if we do not
acknowledge the English Anglican context, but instead consider
them to be Greek Orthodox in translation. The urauthor cannot
receive any name beyond that of the 'Liturgical Commission'.
Knowing the composition and theological preferences of those
on the various committees might help, but it would be impossible
to identify the contribution of individuals. We can though create
a mental image of the origins of the text which will inform our
interpretation. These liturgical texts do have an origin which can be

---

[36]William Irwin, *Intentionalist Interpretation: A Philosophical Explanation and
Defense*, Contributions in Philosophy 73 (Westport: Greenwood Press, 1999),
p. 28.
[37]Ibid., p. 30.
[38]Ibid.

called 'author', if it is impossible to identify separate authors because of the collaborative process, we might use urauthor to denote this multiple and un-nameable (but not anonymous) origin. Irwin's distinctions allow us to retain an author figure as a determinant of meaning, although to what extent does a reader/worshipper need to attend to authorial intentions?

The idea of authorial intention in the text was overthrown by Wimsatt and Beardsley's important paper 'The Intentional Fallacy' published in 1954. They asserted that the author's intention should be restricted to that which is revealed by the text alone, and not by extra-textual factors such as biography and self-critical comment.[39] The text for them is self-revealing and self-contained; it lives in the world on its own terms. Now the author's involvement in the text is only at the point of production, he has no control over its afterlife. Liturgical texts may proffer 'official' meanings, but what worshippers may actually think is only partially related to them; they exercise considerable freedom to suggest for themselves meanings which are 'meaningful' for them. Such freedom from authorial intention could also be illustrated by, for example, nineteenth-century Anglican ritualists interpreting the Book of Common Prayer as consonant with Catholic doctrine and ritual practice; keeping, mostly, the text of the Prayer Book intact, they adopted ritual practices in relation to Real Presence in the Eucharist which distorted the deliberate absence of such a theology in the prayers and rubrics for Holy Communion and in what can be understood of Cranmer's sacramental theology.[40] Such freedom, though, would not be acceptable for a liturgical historian interpreting an historical liturgical text such as the sacramentary of Serapion; historical methodology requires that close attention is paid to the presumed context of composition and performance. Even so, the very diversity of interpretations of this text should alert us to the manner in which the text lives independently of its author, whom we cannot know and whose context we can only dimly appreciate. In liturgical historiography it is not uncommon to encounter a setting-aside

---

[39]W. K. Wimsatt and M. C. Beardsley, 'The Intentional Fallacy', in W. K. Wimsatt (ed.), *The Verbal Icon: Studies in the Meaning of Poetry* (Lexington: University of Kentucky Press, 1954), pp. 3–18.

[40]See Nigel Yates, *Buildings, Faith and Worship* (2nd ed. Oxford: Oxford University Press, 2000), chapter 7.

of the author's context in interpretation when the critical analysis
of scholars is too deeply informed by the liturgical norms of their
own day to produce anachronisms like identifying the prayers after
baptism in the sacramentary as accompanying 'Confirmation'.
If we assert that meaning resides in the text alone, then there are
potentially as many meanings as readers/worshippers, as Stringer
suggested for worship events.[41] What Wimsatt and Beardsley
indicate is that this plurality is a normal condition of textuality and
not a deviation from authorial intention.

Most worshippers, let alone historians, do not rigidly adopt
one or other of these positions but experience meaning-making as
a negotiation between themselves, the text and the author. How
might this happen and what implications does it have for the role
of the author in interpretation? One useful approach might be that
of E. D. Hirsch who distinguished between the author's intention
revealed in the text itself and the interpretation placed upon it by
the reader by separating the 'meaning' and the 'significance' of a
text. The 'meaning' is whatever the author intended and is therefore
fixed at the point of composition; the 'significance', however, is
whatever the reader makes of the text, and that is always going
to be open ended. For the interpretation to be 'validated' though,
the 'significance' should be informed by the establishment of the
meaning intended by the author.[42] This theory does allow us to take
account of the role of the author as an active agent in text production
and accords a status for his intention, while also providing a place
for interpretation by the text's recipient. There is potential here for
investigating the role of authorized liturgical texts in contemporary
churches where a text is produced to conform to a denomination's
theological and/or contextual presuppositions and will display
these intentions in the choice of words and structures, while
allowing for different interpretations when performed in individual
congregations. If we use the Church of England's *Common Worship*
as an example, the two volumes of the *Companion to Common*

[41]Stringer, *Perception*, p. 2 and elsewhere.
[42]E. D. Hirsch, *Validity in Interpretation* (New Haven: Yale University Press, 1967),
discussed in A. Bennett, *The Author* (Abingdon: Routledge, 2005), pp. 78–9.
[43]Paul F. Bradshaw (ed.), *A Companion to Common Worship*, vol. 1, Alcuin Club
Collections 78 (London: SPCK, 2001); vol. 2, Alcuin Club Collections 81 (London:
SPCK, 2006).

Worship[43] might help uncover the 'meaning' contained in the text as the Liturgical Commission intended, but the 'significance' will be that placed upon the text by worship leaders who (ought to) have regard for that 'meaning', and by worshippers who may not. A liturgical text is not an 'intention-free zone', it will have been composed with a specific purpose in mind which cannot be ignored if the text is to have coherence in performance. The intended meaning of the prayer text determines its use and where there are choices to be made, between Eucharistic prayers for example, that choice will be made with regard to the theological 'meaning', but the 'significance' will be expressed ritually or in the minds of the participants.

Conclusion

During a contemporary worship event using a set form of words the author is not normally present as an authoritative interpreter of the text in the way a literary author might be at a literary festival and, by and large, the primary authorial function of text production is hidden; this was not the case when bishops and priests improvised liturgical texts. Ambrose of Milan, for example, may well have exercised his right to improvise the Eucharistic prayer and fortunately his interpretation of the prayer exists in his mystagogical preaching,[44] but such a close connection between the authorial functions of production and meaning are difficult to discern today. In part this is because the worshippers, the readers of text, are so far removed from the production process; texts appear with the disembodied *imprimatur* of a committee or synod and not an individual. However, I am reluctant to abandon authorship as a way of indicating the origin of liturgical texts because it forces us to consider how our texts are created; however, to retain it, 'author' cannot be assigned to an individual, but to the series of functions which Harold Love has described – it designates the processes which cause a text to come into being. Liturgical authors employ

---

[44]Ambrose of Milan, *On the Sacraments* IV.21–8. See Edward J. Yarnold, *The Awe-inspiring Rites of Initiation: The Origins of the RCIA* (Edinburgh: T&T Clark, 1994), pp. 135–9.

the formulae and themes of the liturgical genres, which we shall
discuss in the next chapter, such that originality no longer remains
a dominant characteristic of the authorship of these texts. Authorial
intention also plays a limited role in determining the meaning of a
liturgical text; some regard for the theological and social context of
the liturgical text's production will be necessary for an historical text
and inevitable for a contemporary one, but the reader/worshipper
will not be constrained by intentional meaning when generating its
significance.

3

Genre

In the opening chapter I referred to liturgical 'texts' in an undifferentiated manner, that is with reference to entire liturgical books ('works') or to individual liturgical units; it is to the latter that I shall now turn to examine the, usually implicit, ways in which we distinguish between different types of these units. I intend to demonstrate here that when distinguishing one text from another we subconsciously do so on the basis of genre more than on content, and that genre does not concern the text alone but has embedded in it a particular response available to those who can 'read' the generic indicators, that is to those who are familiar with its use in the worship event.

In daily life, genre is ever-present as one of the ways in which we filter the enormous amount of information which passes before our eyes, but it is rarely the focus of our attention. In broadcast media we distinguish between news, documentary and weather forecasts; each has a language and a way of organizing the information which is conditioned by external factors such as time or the culture of the broadcaster, as much as by the content. Our visits to the bookshop are made more efficient by organizing the books according to their subject: crime, romance, historical, language courses, cookery, etc. Of course these categorizations are based on thematic content, but our ability to appropriate their contents is based to a great extent upon the additional defining feature of how the content is presented. Cookery books will usually present recipes according to a formula in which the list of ingredients comes before the instructions; a biography is normally a chronological account of the hero's life; a grammar book for a foreign language will set out the verbs in a table and not give examples of every mutation in complete

sentences. Through familiarity, these presentational features work
on the reader subconsciously to prepare her mind to receive and
organize the content.

In literary studies, the contemporary move has been away from
genre as a classification system towards attempts to define what
genre is and to elucidate how it functions as part of the meaning-
making process. In liturgical studies, attention to this has been
more limited despite studies of some specific types of liturgical
texts, notably collects and Eucharistic prayers. Here we will
broaden the concerns to provide a more comprehensive picture of
what the liturgical genres might be and how they function in the
worship event, and lastly to look at what happens when the genre
is 'transgressed'. But first to review what genre is and how genres
are distinguished outside the liturgical context.

What is genre?

Historically, and until the recent centuries, works were written to
adhere to specific genres which had existed since Graeco-Roman
times. Aristotle, for example, distinguished 'poiētikē and its
kinds', these were tragedy, comedy, epic and dithyramb (various
lyric forms) but as Donald Russell points out classical genre was
discussed according to general principles and not on the basis of an
existing corpus of literature.[1] The art of good style was to closely
follow the established generic systems, as promoted by Quintillian's
Institutio Oratoria which retained a dominant position until the
renaissance. The primary distinguishing feature of these genres was
the position of the 'speaker' in the work; although modifications of
the core structure might, and did, take place over the centuries, the
classification system endured because of sufficient identity with the
core and peripheral features for there to be 'family resemblance'.[2]
Traditionally too, genre and theme overlapped, such that some
topics could only ever be dealt with in a particular genre; tragedy

[1]Donald A. Russell, *Criticism in Antiquity* (2nd ed. London: Bristol Classical Press,
1995), chapter 10. Here I am reliant on pp. 150–2.
[2]Alastair Fowler, *Kinds of Literature: An Introduction to the Theory of Genres and
Modes* (Oxford: Clarendon Press, 1982), p. 41.

for example, was to present and encourage imitation of an elevated and historical action, whereas comedy would not reflect history or reality.

However, contemporary writing and literary scholarship has shown that both the use and assignment of genre may be based on multiple factors, of which tradition is only one. Assignment of genre to a work may well involve a whole range of features, 'genre indicators', which will apply in some cases but not in others; what in one is a core feature may well be peripheral in another, which makes finding definitions of different genres complex because of the lack of comparability between the classifying features. In his study of genre, Alistair Fowler provided a comprehensive list of these features (or what he calls 'kinds', that is historical genres) which will be useful to recap here as we will recognize many of them when we turn to discuss liturgical genres later.[3] The different factors which may combine to distinguish and assign genre are as follows:

1. Representational aspect: is it narrative, dramatic or discursive?
2. External structure: the organization of content into chapters or stanzas.
3. Metrical structure, a determining feature of classical genres.
4. Size: internal and external constraints on length.
5. Scale: is it broad or focused?
6. Subject: in classical literature certain subjects were confined to a particular manner of expression.
7. Values: the moral world of writer and reader.
8. Mood or emotional coloration.
9. Character occasion.
10. Attitude.
11. *Mis en scène.*
12. Character: the type of characters presented and the depth of personality.
13. The structure of action.

---

[3]Ibid., pp. 60–73.

14 Appropriate style: rhetorical organization; whether elevated, middling or low.

15 The task of the readers: what is required of them to complete the communication.

This list clearly contains items which it would be unusual to apply to liturgical texts – *mis en scène*, for example, but even a brief consideration of familiar texts shows them to be applicable in some cases. Thus if we take 'mood', we can easily note that attention to this criteria allows us to distinguish between doxological and penitential material, but we might also be aware that these moods will not always be accompanied by distinctive representational, external or metrical structures – the psalms frequently combine these. For the criteria of 'scale', we could remark that a prayer to consecrate the Eucharistic elements might encompass the whole of salvation history from creation to the last judgement, but prayers of intercession are often highly localized and particular in focus. We could note that all liturgical texts share common values; that is they are conditioned by the perspective of the kingdom of heaven and not of the world.

Some of Fowler's characteristics do appear in liturgical texts and we can use them, individually and in combination, to help us distinguish and assign the liturgical genres; however, they are a somewhat unwieldy list and more preferable are the three major indicators which John Frow has proposed. These are as follows:[4]

1 Formal organization: the shaping of the material into its external form using the properties of language, of print layout, scale, the time frame and style.

2 Rhetorical structure: the structured relationship between authors and readers; direct or indirect address; the relationship between author and narrator, which may be affected by tone and mood.

3 Thematic content: the actions and actors, recurring topics, argumentation, historicity.

Although Frow is primarily concerned with literary texts which will display a greater number of genres than liturgical texts, it is possible to assign liturgical genre using Frow's three major indicators. Formal organization might be demonstrated by distinguishing prose texts (scripture) from poetry (hymnody), and according to function (e.g. the lectionary from a book of Collects). The rhetorical structure is evident in the indications of who speaks particular texts and to whom they are addressed. Thematic content, for example Lenten texts from Christmas texts, is very easy to detect and thus appears to be a more obvious, albeit deceptive, criteria. These are all familiar genres for those in churches of a liturgical tradition. But what criteria do we use to assign liturgical texts to specific genres; what is the means of classification? By investigating these existing categories we should hopefully arrive at some general features of liturgical genres which will help us further in the chapter when we come to see how these different genres function in the liturgy and how they assist in revealing, or creating, meaning.

Liturgical genres

Even in this preliminary application of genre theory to liturgical texts we can see that genre operates there just as much as in other texts, as a hidden and yet vital part of the production and interpretation of texts. There have been a number of brief attempts to classify types of prayer, although these have not succeeded in bringing into their systems the diversity of liturgical texts.

Origen provides one of the earliest attempts at classification based on theme:

Four topics which I have found scattered throughout the Scriptures appear to me to deserve mention, and according to these everyone should organize their prayer. The topics are as follows: In the beginning and opening of prayer, glory is to be ascribed according to one's ability to God, through Christ who is to be glorified with Him, and in the Holy Spirit who is to be proclaimed with Him. Thereafter, one should put thanksgivings: common thanksgivings – into which he introduces benefits conferred upon men in general – and thanksgivings for things which he has personally received from God. After thanksgiving it appears to me that one ought to become a powerful accuser of one's own sins before God and ask first for healing with a view to being released from the habit which brings on sin, and secondly for forgiveness for past actions. After confession it appears to me that one ought to append as a fourth element the asking for the great and heavenly things, both personal and general, on behalf of one's nearest and dearest. And last of all, one should bring prayer to an end ascribing glory to God through Jesus Christ in the Holy Spirit.[5]

So following Origen, prayers can be differentiated according to whether they were supplicatory, intercessory, thanksgiving, etc., although he says nothing about the formal organization or rhetorical structure of these, which, as he here presumes private oral prayer, is unsurprising.

Modern commentators have turned to other criteria and discuss prayer in relation to written or printed texts. Louis Duchesne identified three 'forms' of common prayer: 'litany' prayers, 'collective' prayers and 'eucharistic' prayers.[6] He does not directly explain his reasons for classifying prayer in these ways but does indicate the differences between them as primarily concerning the manner in which the minister and congregation interact. Thus he says, that litany prayers involve the specification of different needs to which the congregation responds by a short supplication; collective prayers include the collects (which we shall discuss below) and are distinguished by a formula of invitation to pray, the adoption of a silent and appropriate attitude on the part of the congregation, the pronouncement of a formula or resumé and concluding with a congregational 'Amen'; Eucharistic prayers are offered by the minister alone in the name of the whole congregation, they open with a set dialogue and contain the theme of a general thanksgiving. For Duchesne, the primary genre indicator is the addressivity of the text, that is its rhetorical structure: genre is not related to thematic content, nor even the text's position in the liturgy.

Kathleen Hughes undertook a more comprehensive analysis by attempting to provide a taxonomy of prayer and almost achieved

---

[5]Origen, *On Prayer* 20. <http://www.ccel.org/ccel/origen/prayer.xxi.html> [accessed 29 March 2012].
[6]Louis Duchesne, *Christian Worship: Its Origin and Evolution*, 5th ed. translated by M. L. McClure (London: SPCK, 1923), p. 106.

a biological model or family tree of prayer.[7] She also based her classification upon rhetorical structure and her primary genre indicator is the communication pattern. Prayer types are differentiated by the nature and direction of the president's address: formal or informal; to God or to the people; with the people or for the people; or even by himself for himself. Her principal category is simply called 'liturgical prayer' for which the common structural feature seems only to be the concluding assent of the congregation by 'Amen'; branching out from this, she identified seven subcategories which themselves are further subdivided (genre and subgenres, perhaps). Here, neither formal organization nor thematic content are the key characteristics which lead to genre assignment but rather the structures of address, which, almost uniquely of all the attempts to categorize liturgical prayer, results in no overlap between the lower categories.

It does seem that there is an emerging consensus that rhetorical structure is a key criterion for the principal liturgical genre of prayer, but clearly worshippers encounter more than prayers among their liturgical texts. I will not attempt to match Hughes by proposing a taxonomy of liturgical texts but will draw attention to the diversity of liturgical genres. In doing so, I will presume some familiarity with the sort of texts to be encountered in modern Western Eucharistic worship and which are found in the liturgical books of the historic and liturgical churches.

Returning briefly to the model provided by the classical genres, it is possible at the simplest level to assign three principal genres to liturgical texts: that is, prose, poetry and prayer, and then to further determine subgenres as subsidiaries of these. The liturgical genres could be categorized as follows:

prose – scriptural readings, sermon, or introductory statements

poetry – psalmody, hymns, canticles, anthems, choruses

prayer – collects, eucharistic prayers, blessings, intercessions, litanies.

Reflecting further on what it is that distinguishes these three, we find that thematic content and addressivity can transcend the

---

[7]Kathleen Hughes, 'Prayer, Types of, in the Liturgy' in Peter E. Fink (ed.), *The New Dictionary of Sacramental Theology* (Collegeville: The Liturgical Press, 1990), pp. 959–67.

categories and so what remains are some very generalized, although serviceable, core genre indicators. Using Frow's three categories we shall explore these in a more detailed manner.

The first of Frow's generic indicators is formal organization, that is how the text is presented on the page and where it might be located. Liturgical books distinguish between prose on the one hand and poetry and prayer on the other: the former is presented in paragraphs, while poetry and prayer are presented in broken lines and in stanzas. These features communicate to the one charged with reading them aloud how the text is to be read, where to pause for breath, and in some cases where inflection can aid the reception of meaning. Worshippers are also familiar with the provision of specific books for each genre: although psalms and canticles might be contained within a liturgical book intended for congregational use, hymns, choruses and anthems are usually placed in separate books. Similarly many prose texts are not contained in the liturgical book: the scripture readings will be read from a complete Bible or a Lectionary or Book of Gospels and the like; sermons, with the exception of the Anglican *Book of Homilies* and for the Orthodox John Chrysostom's Easter sermon, are unlikely to be circulated before their delivery – these texts are not part of the liturgical books. Unsurprisingly, then, 'Prayer Books' contain mostly prayers!

There is though one problematic text whose formal organization can cause genre confusion. The creeds, Apostles' and Nicene-Constantinopolitan, are almost always presented in broken lines even though they were intended as prose texts. Here, the formal organization serves to assist the performance of this liturgical unit, it aids the sense of the text by formally indicating pauses and stops and this is appropriate for a text which is customarily recited by the whole congregation. When, however, the creed is sung, these external presentational features turn it from a statement of belief into something approaching a hymn and, additionally, interpretation will be affected by the style of musical setting. With some settings it can appear as a recapitulation of the Gloria which blurs the distinction between a hymn of praise and a doctrinal statement. As this example shows performance can be an unreliable way of determining liturgical genres.

Liturgical poetry is divided into subgenres according to the external feature of metre and by its source. Psalmody is only ever taken from the biblical psalter, it has an irregular metre, or rather no metre at all in translation; canticles are biblical, also unmetred, but not from the psalter; hymnody is almost never from scripture, although may be inspired by it, and is always metrical; anthems can be biblical or non-biblical, metred or non-metred and these are often characterized by who sings them. Psalmody might also be identified by its location in the liturgy and the manner of singing it – that is, it can be sung antiphonally, as can canticles, but hymns and choruses are never sung like this. Authority is also a determining factor: psalms and canticles are scriptural, hymns have the authority of tradition, but choruses being contemporary, informal and ephemeral have limited authority. Hymns and choruses may change with fashion, but scriptural poetry is always retained. Our examination of liturgical poetry provides us with some new genre indicators: authority, use, external presentation, manner of performing and speaker. What is not a characteristic of this genre and its subgenres is thematic content or mood: they may be doxological, or penitential, or for thanksgiving but none of these are strong genre indicators. This is also the case for the other principal liturgical genres of prose and prayer where again thematic content may not be a strong generic indicator, but rather we need to look at external features.

Turning to rhetorical structure, we could distinguish liturgical genres and subgenres by the relationship established between speaker(s) and addressee, and by tone and mood. It is in prayer, particularly, that addressivity becomes a key indicator. The genre of prayer is distinguished from the other liturgical genres by its exclusive addressivity to God (notwithstanding intercessory petitions to saints in some traditions); it is never the genre used for address within the congregation between minister and people or between people. Whereas prose may be addressed to God, to individuals or to the whole congregation, and poetry may be addressed to God or simply be about God, prayer is exclusively addressed to 'you' or 'Thou', in distinction to the use of 'you' or 'Ye' to denote the congregation.[8] The position of the speaker is not determinative for this genre, it could be I or we, except in so far that prayer is always addressed from the first person. Subgenres of prayer may be determined by thematic content, that is prayers of penitence, of intercession, of thanksgiving (as Origen) regardless

---

[8]Here contemporary English is hampered by insufficient pronouns.

of the way in which these themes are expressed; or they may be determined by structure alone regardless of the thematic content (i.e. collects and litanies). Context too is important, an exclamation of 'Oh God' uttered outside the context of worship is almost never the genre indicator for prayer!

We have considered addressivity as a key element in identifying prayer genres, but whereas Hughes looked at the way the leader and congregation address each other and only then turned to the structure of prayers, a more nuanced approach would require the listing of a variety of genre indicators not all of which would be evident in every example of that genre. This further emphasizes the problem with the taxonomic or biological model as it is normally predicated upon a single indicator which it then struggles to apply to every instance. Prayers can be differentiated by the manner in which they are communicated and by structure and by thematic content; however, as we shall see in relation to the highly structured collect, thematic content is a very weak indicator.

Commentators emphasize the social nature of genres in that within them are embedded a whole range of relationships. In literature this is most evident in the presence or absence of the authorial voice in a work and the assumptions made about the relationship between this voice and the reader. In liturgy too, liturgical units have different 'authorial voices'; they may be spoken by 'I' which could be an individual or could be the whole community, by the minister on behalf of the whole church, or on behalf of God; by 'we' which could be everyone, or the minister on behalf of everyone, or indeed everyone except an individual or group; or they may be in the third person and/or use a passive voice. Liturgical genres are distinguished by the voice and the addressee. Prose texts, except the sermon, usually involve some sort of ventriloquism or deferred authority: even if these units contain 'I' or 'we', the authorial voice is not the same as the one speaking. So readings are attributed to Isaiah, Matthew or Paul; introductory prefaces in the BCP are an address by the Church to the people. In prayer and poetry, the speakers of these texts speak them as if they were the authorial voice, regardless of whether they are addressed to God ('you'), or are about God ('he').

Frow's third genre indicator was thematic content. In literature the reader can anticipate the manner in which a plot may unfold if she knows she is reading crime fiction or an autobiography. In these genres the indicators are inextricably bound up with the thematic content; however, in liturgical texts what we have noticed so far is how thematic content has very little role in the use and interpretation of genre. Poetry, prose and prayer may all express thanksgiving, anamnesis, contrition or praise; no one theme is reserved for a single genre. And in many liturgical rites a theme for the whole service will be reflected in many different texts during the rite. Worshippers will not necessarily use the theme to anticipate their response to a liturgical text, but rather use more overt genre indicators based on rhetorical structure.

A liturgical subgenre: The collect

The collect is one of the few kinds of liturgical text to have received scholarly attention because its genre indicators are so strong and have endured for centuries. A collect has a distinctive formal organization and rhetorical structure which permits the expression of a very broad range of themes. Unlike some of the texts referred to above, the collect is identified not just by textual elements, but also by the distinctive manner of its performance.

On the whole there is reasonable consensus about the basic structure of a collect and this table (Table 3.1) summarizes the principal commentators.

Notable here is that the collect genre contains elements which stand outside the prayer itself – the invitation to pray and the period of silence. It is interesting that the congregational 'Amen' seems to be missing from the structures provided by some commentators, although that too is a key element. The prayer organizes and reveals the point of the prayer, that is the petition, in a distinctive way; it follows a laudatory address to God and precedes a justification for the request. Composers of collects write them to adhere to the genre indicators and in the worship event, worshippers are expected to 'get' the meaning by anticipating that each line of the prayer will follow the standard pattern. The meaning and the structure are intertwined. The genre indicator also operates upon the worshipper at the level of performance: 'Let us pray' is never an indication to utter the prayer together with the minister and worshippers prepare to perform their 'Amen' during the doxology.

TABLE 3.1 *The stable generic features of a collect*

Duchesne, 1923[a]	Jungmann, 1949 (1958)[b]	Willis, 1968[c]	Hughes, 1990[d]
President invites faithful to pray	Invitation to pray and/ or assume appropriate posture		
Congregation assume silent attitude of prayer			Adequate silence
	Address to God	Address to God	Address to God
	'Relative predication'	Relative or participle clause referring to some attribute of God, or one of his saving acts	Amplification of the address
	Petition commencing with *et* and following previous clause	The petition	Petition
		The reason for which we ask	(The reason for asking)
		The conclusion	Concluding doxology
Congregation assent with 'Amen'			

[a]Duchesne, *Christian Worship*, p. 107.
[b]Joseph A. Jungmann, *The Mass of the Roman Rite, Its Origins and Development*, translated by Francis A. Brunner (London: Burns and Oates, 1959), pp. 249–50.
[c]G. G. Willis, *Further Essays in Early Roman Liturgy*, Alcuin Club Collections vol. 50 (London: SPCK, 1968), p. 118.
[d]Hughes, 'Prayer', pp. 959–67.

In this subgenre, information (the narrative if you like) is revealed according to a particular structure and seemingly does so regardless of the content or even the period in which it was composed. If we look at collects in the *Verona Sacramentary*, or the Sarum rite, or BCP or the Tridentine Rite, and then from our own times the 1969 *Roman Missal*, the US Episcopal Church's 1979 Book of Common Prayer, the list could go on, we can see that collects composed in different eras for different ecclesial communities, in different social and cultural milieu follow the conventions of this subgenre. Even the avowedly creative Iona Community use the same structure in their office books:

O Christ, the Master Carpenter,
who at the last, through wood and nails,
purchased our whole salvation.
Wield well your tools in the workshop of your world,
so that we who come rough-hewn to your bench
may here be fashioned to a truer beauty of your hand.
We ask it for your name's sake.
AMEN[9]

Function is a contested indicator for the 'collect'. Jungmann assigned the collect to the start of the Mass when the priest addresses the congregation for the first time and so it functions as a summary, a collecting together, of all the themes evident in the entry rituals;[10] in the Anglican tradition and in the modern Roman rite, although it remains as part of the opening rites, it has been connected to the readings and thus sums up the theme of the day which the readings will then elaborate. We also note that the collect genre is used for prayers after Communion, once again structure and performance dominate the genre indicators, so too might mood, while the thematic content varies considerably.

A similar point could be made about the anaphoral subgenre, which also displays clear common and peripheral structural features but, in

[9]Iona Abbey, *Worship Book* (Glasgow: Wild Goose Publications, 2001), p. 19. See also the prayers of Janet Morley in *All Desires Known* (3rd ed. London: SPCK, 2005), which bring new themes and metaphors to traditional structures.
[10]Jungmann, *The Mass of the Roman Rite*, p. 241.

distinction to the collect, also displays common and peripheral thematic elements. Recent Eucharistic compositions by Western churches have rarely done anything radical to either the structure or thematic content of these prayers, but have simply selected from the menu of traditional elements and themes. This should alert us to the enduring nature of genres for liturgical composition and performance. Despite changes from Latin to forms of the vernacular, from renaissance English to modern American or Australasian English, it is the generic indicators which persist. One would be tempted therefore to argue that, in liturgical worship, the truly archaic and therefore traditional feature is genre, not language.

Genre transgression

Genre transgression is the deliberate rejection or subversion of the indicators anticipated of a particular genre and, as Fowler comments, for there to be transgression the norms must be already well established.[11] The shift in many protestant churches away from historic patterns of worship, and even from a compulsion to use the prescribed formulae, and a promotion or tolerance of 'creative' liturgy has brought accusations of transgression from liturgists and worshippers alike. But what really is being transgressed? Surely not worship itself, but rather the texts which facilitate the worship. The Iona community collect cited above indicates that even the most creative liturgical community may not really transgress genre, even though the thematic content is unusual; most commonly liturgical revision and innovation is based on language style and content.

Liturgical genres may be transgressed or transformed through purposed creativity and some contemporary liturgical material has deliberately chosen to ignore generic conventions. An interesting example is the dialogue Eucharistic prayer, for which examples can be found in the Roman Catholic second Eucharistic prayer for use with children or in Eucharistic Prayer H of *Common Worship*. Dialogue is a common feature of liturgical worship where it is used without comment in the *Sursum Corda*[12] and in litanies. The genre

---

[11]Fowler, *Kinds of Literature*, p. 93.

[12]The name usually given to the whole opening dialogue of the Eucharistic prayer, but which, in fact, only refers to the petition 'Lift up your hearts'.

indicators of liturgical dialogue could be expressed as its distinctive manner of address, where the congregation assent using prescribed words to what is usually given as a proposition by the minister. Thus 'Lift up your hearts' is followed by response 'We lift them to the Lord'; in the litany, petitions are assented to by the responses 'Lord have mercy' or 'Grant this O lord'. (We note only too easily how the formal language of a liturgical dialogue distinguishes it from conversational dialogue, or a television interview.) What happens when these genre indicators are juxtaposed with those of the anaphora? In the example of the Roman Catholic prayer for use with children, several opening declarations of praise spoken by the priest are confirmed by the congregation singing the Sanctus after each section; the epiclesis with a form of the Benedictus; the institution narrative with 'Jesus has given his life for us'; and the anamnesis, offering and intercessions with 'We praise you, we bless you, we thank you'.[13] There is here minimal disruption to the structuring of the thematic content of the anaphoral genre so that the congregation's response is more of a refrain than a distinctive contribution.[14] The transgression concerns the performance of the text, but it is quite modest compared to those in which the congregation make a *contribution* to the praying of the Eucharistic prayer. In Prayer H of *Common Worship*, for example, the congregation speaks parts of the constitutive elements of the Eucharistic prayer which are normally reserved for the priest. Thus after the institution narrative, the prayer continues:

> As we proclaim his death and celebrate his rising in glory,
> send your Holy Spirit that this bread and this wine
> may be to us the body and blood of your dear Son.

> *All* **As we eat and drink these holy gifts**
> **make us one in Christ, our risen Lord.**[15]

---

[13]Eucharistic Prayer for use with Children II § 4–5, 7–8. Roman Catholic Church, *Eucharistic Prayers for Masses with Children, for Use with the Roman Missal* (3rd ed. Dublin: Veritas, 2013), pp. 22–5.

[14]This distinction is clearly shown by dialogues such as 'The Lord be with you/and also with you'.

[15]*CW*, p. 205. The entire text of all *Common Worship* books can be viewed on the Church of England website <http://www.churchofengland.org/prayer-worship/worship/texts.aspx> [accessed 29 March 2012].

The transgressive element here concerns the rhetorical structure of the prayer, in that it is no longer addressed to God by the priest on behalf of the people, but addressed to God by the whole people.

What is the effect of such transgressions or transformations of the anaphoral genre? In the first instance, that of assent, the transformation is relatively superficial; the structural and thematic characteristics have not been changed, neither has the relationship between worshippers, minister and God, it merely enhances the element of assent which is already part of this genre. In the case of the addition of a refrain, the increased participation does nothing to alter the power and social structures of the prayer. It may disturb the structuring of content in the prayer by disrupting the disclosure of the narrative as the refrain may not always relate directly to that which immediately precedes and succeeds it. The fully participatory prayer attempts a democratization of the liturgical functions that has more to do with theologies of ministry than anything else. These prayers do look radical on the page, but have more implications for social and hierarchical relations in the congregation. Nevertheless they do retain the key structural and thematic genre indicators; however, considering that embedded in any particular genre is a set of relationships between speakers and listeners, then these are transgressive enough.

If all worship is transgressive in as much as it moves the participant from membership of the kingdom of this world to membership of the kingdom of God, then for some communities that has signalled that the means of worship should also transgress tradition and authority. Such liturgies may be sought from individuals and communities who put themselves outside traditional ecclesial structures – an extreme case might be the complete rejection of liturgical worship by the Society of Friends hand in hand with the hierarchical ordering which may also accompany it. Others have sought new liturgical material using a specific theological motif which is transgressive in light of tradition, that is, Feminist, Queer, Peace and Justice, etc. The liturgical outworking of these have often resulted in a challenge to patriarchy which has affected language and performance. Language has been altered to remove unnecessary masculine nouns and pronouns, and in performance liturgical leadership has become diffused and participatory. Despite this, and the great explosion of new liturgical material over the last twenty or thirty years, the modest changes in thematic content and addressivity have not greatly troubled the traditional liturgical genres.

Encountering genre

In a Eucharistic liturgy we distinguish between prayer, readings, hymnody, sermon and within these between different types of prayers, readings from different parts of scripture and non-scriptural sources, metrical and non-metrical poetry. But genre works on us unconsciously during worship: worshippers pick up generic clues by experience, what we might call 'liturgical competence', which enables them to identify the generic code at the beginning of a liturgical unit. Sometimes the generic indicator will be very explicit and in the form of an instruction, thus 'Let us pray . . .' or 'A reading from the gospel according to . . .'. Elsewhere, worshippers develop a familiarity with where particular texts occur in the liturgy and the conventions of communal worship indicate appropriate physical and mental responses to them. Knowledge of the generic code or correct identification of the clues/generic indicators prepare the worshipper for an appropriate attitude, posture or response. This is self-evident from penitential liturgical units which engender a spirit of quiet contrition in the congregation, the readings a quiet attentiveness, but a more 'upbeat' spirit of thanksgiving and praise in post-communion prayers. Worshippers do not need to be told to adopt these attitudes, postures or responses; they are generated by the liturgical units themselves, and further it is not the content which produces this response, but it is anticipated on the basis of genre recognition. In this way it is possible to change the thematic content of a liturgical unit without restricting the worshippers' ability to respond appropriately because the generic indicators are strong enough to enable that appropriate response. So each Sunday there is a different collect, proper preface, Eucharistic prayer, post-communion prayer, hymns, and readings, but the performed response of worshippers to each one is the same each week because they recognize each specific genre.

In discussing genre so far we have been interested in its external manifestation, but studies into the reception of genre shifts our understanding of it as a tool for authors into a tool for readers or worshippers. When encountering a text for the first time, the reader will already have a store of knowledge about the genre even if they are unsure about the content. Thus Hans Jauss has said that because every work belongs to a genre, it will have 'a preconstituted horizon of expectation ... ready at hand ... to orientate the reader's (public's) understanding and to enable a qualifying reception'.[16] When choosing a genre, the writer or speaker makes a presumption about the background knowledge held by the reader or listener, who in turn needs that knowledge to fully reveal the meaning in the text. So the reader either approaches a text knowing the genre, in which case he will anticipate a particular ordering of information, or he will pick up the genre indicators as he reads and then use his experience of genre to make sense of the contents and meaning. Once we pick up the clue to the genre we are able to interpret a text more fully. As Frow describes, 'Genre cues act rather like context-sensitive drop-down menus in a computer program, directing me to the layers and sub-layers of information that respond to my purposes as a speaker, or a reader or a viewer.'[17]

The analysis of specific liturgical units can enable us to reveal something about how structured and linguistic features are triggers or generic indicators, and demonstrate the stability of liturgical genres through time. Liturgical texts exhibit a purposed archaism which is not dissimilar to classical and renaissance uses of genre. It is clear from recent liturgical revisions that the traditional liturgical genres have been retained despite changes in thematic content and language style. The use of a particular genre or subgenre indicates a desire to convey meaning through structure just as much as through thematic content. This is most evident in the adoption of the generic indicators of Eucharistic prayers for prayers over the water in some contemporary liturgical rites.[18] The indicators of the Eucharistic prayer (or anaphoral) subgenre which is evident by an opening dialogue, a thanksgiving preface leading to anamnesis, epiclesis

---

[16]Hans Robert Jauss, 'Theory of Genres and Medieval Literature' in David Duff, *Modern Genre Theory* (Harlow: Longman, 2000), p. 131. Jauss's article first appeared in *Toward an Aesthetic of Reception* (Minneapolis: University of Minnesota, 1982 [1970]), pp. 76–109.
[17]Frow, *Genre*, p. 84.
[18]See the prayers of blessing over the water in the Roman Catholic 'Rite for the Christian Initiation of Adults', or in *Common Worship: Christian Initiation*, or in 'Baptism 2' of the *Book of Common Prayer* of the Church in Ireland (2004).

and doxology, alert the worshippers to sacramental action and the choice of this subgenre by the liturgical commission is a response to the more widespread reassertion of the importance of baptism. Thus, as Frow suggests, a genre conveys more information than that carried by the thematic content.

Conclusion

This discussion of genre sends us back to review our previous two chapters on textuality and authorship; although genre may be found in other media, the way it functions in liturgical texts is similar to other texts. Liturgical genre is a result of liturgical textuality – which we can most obviously see in the use of a relative clause in the collect. Contemporary liturgical authors, by and large unconsciously, fashion their texts using the known principal genres of poetry, prose and prayer; however, they self-consciously model new liturgical material upon the existing subgenres, especially those for prayer. The liturgical authors pre-exist as worshippers, and participation in worship has conditioned them to instinctively seek out specific subgenres to convey particular messages at appropriate points in the liturgy. The pervasiveness of genre shows once more the limitations on liturgical authors who are constrained by inherited conventions and by the expectations of worshippers. Worshippers use genre as a tool to reveal the meaning of texts; the not-always self-conscious identification of a liturgical genre will cause them to prepare themselves to hear the text – they prepare their mood, their attentiveness, their expectation of the way in which the message will be conveyed. Understanding how liturgical genre functions, then, is one more tool for understanding the processes of text production and interpretation.

4

Narrative

In this chapter, I want to focus our attention upon the narrative features of liturgical worship and how narrative is used in liturgical and para-liturgical texts.[1] We encounter narrative more overtly in novels, television dramas, films and plays, but those working in narrative theory have extended the application of a narrative interpretation to non-fiction texts, as well as to how we understand ourselves as humans. This last aspect is important in relation to liturgical worship and I shall start by reflecting upon narrative as an essential component of self-understanding and relate it to the impact of worship on the process of self-formation. As our discussion in each chapter moves us ever closer to the consideration about how the text functions in worship, which will be the focus of our final chapter, narrative is a good place to start thinking about how the liturgical text operates beyond the surface of the text. But the purpose of the book is to base our observations upon that surface of the text, and so for the remainder of the chapter I shall explore how the different elements of narrative (plot, character, etc.) are present in liturgical texts and conclude with a narrative reading of a contemporary Eucharistic prayer.

Narrative and self[2]

If asked to say who we are, it would be fairly unsurprising to begin with the story of our life; we take it for granted in ordinary

---

[1]By 'para-liturgical texts' I mean texts which discuss liturgical texts, rather than provide material for the act of worship itself, that is homilies, commentaries, etc.
[2]See my 'Stories of Self and Salvation at Baptism', *Anaphora* 1, no. 2 (2007), pp. 37–52. Much of this opening section is taken from that article which further develops the theme in relation to the transformation effected by baptism.

social contexts that the listener to our story will gain an insight, not only into the formative experiences of our past, but that they will understand how we perceive ourselves to be in the present, and also what may inspire our future life. Stanley Hauerwas and David Burrell have suggested that we have a 'categorical preference for story over explanation as a vehicle of understanding'.[3] In telling our story we are likely to recall moments of great change, crisis or reorientation but, despite that, in both the telling and the reception of our narrative an identical subject would be recognized. The events of a story happen in time, but we would want to assert the continuity of our selves despite the progression of time; this Alasdair MacIntyre has called 'psychological continuity'.[4] And Stephen Crites has further described this continuity: 'Our sense of personal identity depends upon the continuity of experience through time, a continuity bridging even the cleft between remembered past and projected future . . . our sense of ourselves is at every moment to some extent integrated into a single story.'[5] Our story will also be dependent upon the linguistic and cultural environments of ourselves and of the enquirer; so, additionally, the context of our narrative is determinative of how we perceive ourselves.

Paul Ricoeur and Alasdair MacIntyre would claim that narrative reflects the narrative order of experience. Thus, our self-identity is shaped by events, perceptions and reflections, and narrative serves to render coherent our disparate experiences; there cannot be a non-narrative reality.[6] Is it possible to know ourselves independently of the narrative we construct for ourselves? It is difficult to conceive how we could. This narrative is not just a device with which I organize my sense of self, but it is the only means by which I can know myself.

---

[3]Stanley Hauerwas and David Burrell, 'From System to Story: An Alternative Pattern for Rationality in Ethics', in Stanley Hauerwas and L. Gregory Jones (eds), *Why Narrative? Readings in Narrative Theology* (Grand Rapids: Eerdmans, 1989), p. 184.
[4]Alasdair MacIntyre, *After Virtue, A Study in Moral Theology* (London: Duckworth, 1985), p. 217.
[5]Stephen Crites, 'The Narrative Quality of Experience', in Hauerwas and Jones, *Why Narrative?*, p. 78.
[6]See Andreea Deciu Ritivoi, 'Identity and Narrative', in David Herman, Manfred Jahn and Marie-Laure Ryan (eds), *Routledge Encyclopedia of Narrative Theory* (London: Routledge, 2005), p. 231.

But, how do we distinguish the narrative we tell about and to ourselves from the other narratives in which we find ourselves, or which relate to our own? Jean-François Lyotard distinguished and explored the relationship between *grand récits*, the metanarrative which dominates any cultural epoch, from the *petits récits*, our personal stories.[7] To what extent am I determined by the metanarrative? This is an important issue in relation to the effect of liturgical worship upon the self: how is my narrative determined by the narrative of salvation recalled in worship? Hauerwas and Burrell suggest that the adoption of different stories enables us to become different people: 'In allowing ourselves to adopt and be adopted by a particular story we are . . . assuming a set of practices which will shape the ways we relate to ourselves and our destiny.'[8] MacIntyre refers to my narrative being '*embedded* in the story of those communities from which I derive my identity'.[9] At its simplest, an embedded narrative is 'a story within a story' – participation in the liturgy permits me to embed my narrative in the narrative of salvation.

My past is constructed of experiences in the form of events in which I have participated or observed, perceptions received through the senses and reasoned reflections upon both these. In recalling my experiences, perceptions and reflections I do not simply list them as items in a chronicle, rather I construct from them an autobiography, a provisional and incomplete account of myself in which I present both my inner and public life. Despite the discontinuities in such a narrative, it does display the constancy of the self as subject. What unites my lived past as I recall and reconstruct it, the past of my community and the different selves I may present in different contexts is the unity of my life. I cannot change my lived past, even though I may recall it differently depending upon circumstances, and at different stages of my life the significant features of my narrative are more than likely to change.

Charlotte Linde[10] has shown that, despite the opportunities for the random selection of events, perceptions and reflections in the

---

[7]Jean-François Lyotard, *The Postmodern Condition: A Report on Knowledge*, translated by *Geoff Bennington and Brian Massumi* (Minneapolis: University of Minnesota Press, 1984).
[8]Hauerwas and Burrell, 'From System to Story', p. 186.
[9]MacIntyre, *After Virtue*, p. 221.
[10]Charlotte Linde, *Life Stories: The Creation of Coherence* (New York: Oxford University Press, 1993).

construction of narratives, despite digression and memory loss, narrators employ a variety of 'coherence structures', which may be 'themes or plots along which the individual can articulate a systematic sense of self'.[11] The narrative does not have to achieve the standards of truth which one might associate with a reputable news agency, but it does need to contain sufficient identity with the narrator for the readers or listeners recognize that the subject is one and the same self. She asserts that it is we ourselves who require that our narrative have coherence:

> adequate coherence is also a personal demand that we make on ourselves. Just as the life story . . . as a social unit has some correspondence to an internal, private story, so the coherence that we produce for social consumption bears a relation to our own individual desire to understand our life as coherent, as making sense, as the history of a proper person . . . most of the time we manage to maintain coherence . . . quite adequately. Nonetheless we can become aware of this personal demand for coherence in situations where some new event has happened that we do not know how to form into a narrative, since it does not fit into our life story.[12]

In each new experience or perception I am not made anew, the unity of my self is maintained by my role as the subject of the narrative, even though I acknowledge that I may undergo quite fundamental changes which cause a reconstruction of previous narratives of my past and possible future. Understanding ourselves narratively enables us to identify a unity despite these changes, as well as acknowledging that we may undergo development in time. Recognition of our self occurs in the telling of our story but at any moment we chose events, people and interpretations to suit the context in which the story is told. The aim of our storytelling is to create 'coherence' – by telling it in the present, the choices we make are determined by the context of the telling.[13] The narrative which

[11]Ritivoi, 'Identity and Narrative', p. 234.
[12]Linde, *Life Stories*, p. 17.
[13]This is well illustrated by the similarity in structure and content of the conversion stories which Martin Stringer noted in the independent evangelical church (*Perception*, pp. 153–9).

we tell ourselves and others needs to have coherence, otherwise it ceases to be about our self and does not draw together the various events, perceptions and reflections. As I have argued elsewhere, after baptism the self can only have coherence if we join the narrative of Christ and of salvation history to our own narrative, and this narrative is reinforced at every worship event through the telling of Christ's story and through our own immersion in that narrative through ritual and text.[14]

Narrative and text

So to move from the necessity of narrative for self-construction to the characteristics of narrative specifically related to texts. What is a narrative? At its simplest, the relating of something which may or may not have happened, it involves characters and ideas, a time sequence, an ordering of events – a beginning, middle and end. Investigating the nature of narrative in texts and the means which the author uses to tell the story will be investigated here in relation to texts more generally, especially fictional texts, as a precursor to applying the ideas to a liturgical text.

When we use the word 'narrative', we generally indicate by it some sort of storytelling. Narrative presumes the presence of a narrator, the one who tells the story; it presumes the story itself; and a recipient of the story, sometimes called the 'narratee'. Such a simple linear outline, though, does not get us very far when we consider the complexity of narratives which we encounter in books, plays and films. A narrative may well have a narrator, but outside autobiography it would be a mistake to equate the narrator with the author. The narrator may tell the story to a narratee, but again we cannot equate the immediate recipient of the story with us as readers or viewers. The power of the author in this regard needs to be appreciated as it is he who selects the story for the narrator, who controls the release of information, who adopts a perspective

---

[14]Here Graham Hughes' comments on the dissonance between the narratives of secular and religious life displayed by some fundamentalist Christians is useful. See his *Worship as Meaning: A Liturgical Theology for Late Modernity* (Cambridge: Cambridge University Press, 2003), pp. 233–44.

and character for the narrator. Even if the author presents the narrator as omniscient, that is apparently standing outside the story and relating it as if from a bird's eye view, what the narrator tells us may well not be the whole story and it is highly unlikely to represent the author's own inclinations in real life. By separating what happens within the text between the narrator and narratee from what happens outside the text between author and reader, we can become aware of the ways in which the story is presented to us and to reflect upon the devices used in constructing it.

A basic constituent of the act of narration is the presumption of a recipient for the story. In the immediate context of a story there may be a designated narattee ('Dear diary . . . '), but the author writes for an audience outside the text, who might be called the implied/ideal/ postulated reader. Additionally, there is the real reader, that is us. The recipient of a narrative may well be part of the story, or used as a device to enable the story to be told. The reader is someone else; we may stand outside the telling and receiving of the story as ones who witness the exchange, but nevertheless we do participate in interpreting it. We contribute to the story by imagining it, we have to make the world of the story come alive – to engage in 'world making'.[15]

In a narrative, events are connected in a related way, which distinguishes it from a chronicle. They may not contain every piece of information but, where there are gaps, the art of authorship and of reading is to fill those gaps with credible continuations of the story. The relationship between events is indicated by the manner in which one event is presented so as to cause or explain another. The events are meaningfully connected and this connectedness is what we might call the 'plot'. So a narrative has the story, the events and a plot, the way the events have been linked.

Characters act out the events: they can be 'rounded', that is displaying a rather full series of psychological characteristics; or flat, that is simply cameos, playing supporting roles. The story is told through their actions, words and thoughts. We may not necessarily identify with them or find them sympathetic, and our

---

[15]For a concise and comprehensive discussion of this topic, see Gerald Prince, 'Reader', in *The Living Handbook of Narratology* (Hamburg University Press, 2011) <http://hup.sub.uni-hamburg.de/lhn/index.php/Reader#Definition> [accessed 29 March 2012].

reaction to them will in part be determined by the way in which they are presented and by our own personal response to the type of character being portrayed. However, the story lives in these characters and their ability to create for us a credible world which we can inhabit in our imagination.

Stories conventionally have a 'beginning, middle and end' and thus we recognize the role of time in the narrative. The story may not be presented in chronological time, it may start in the middle and leave the beginning up to the imagination, or it may be without an end and leave us unsatisfied or curious for the next instalment. The narrative too has a time – the amount of time it takes to tell the story – and it will move at different speeds: dialogue appears to happen in real time; in description, time seems to stand still as there is no action and the story does not move on; there may be repetitions; it may linger over important information and skip over the superficial or unnecessary.

The manner of telling the story can indicate to us the means which we will need to interpret it, or to make a world from it. Genre is an important tool and, as we have indicated in the previous chapter, we implicitly distinguish between genres because of our experience as readers, and we bring to each known genre a set of presuppositions about how material will be presented so that we can employ the appropriate means to unpack the meaning of a text. Genre can determine the ordering of the story, the complexity of the characters, the amount and style of dialogue, etc. Narratives are organized then according to genre conventions, of which chronology is only one feature. Conventions of presentation and organization will accompany each genre: division into chapters, acts and episodes are also tools to aid comprehension.

Our ability to make sense of a story is determined by the level of coherence in its telling, or by the provision of sufficient clues to enable us to fill in gaps, deliberate or unintentional, in the story. For a story to be credible it should display coherence. That does not mean that in every case it must be identical to everyday life but, within the world created by the story, the events and characters are credible. It is possible to have a dissonant narrative where, as a deliberate strategy, the author allows the narrator to present a version of events which other clues tell us is not what the story is at all.

It is becoming clear by now that a distinction can be made between the story and the way it is told. When we are immersed in a story we rarely notice the manner of its presentation, but if we use the tools of narrative theory we cannot avoid paying attention to the way in which the story is told. We become consciously aware of the discourse level of the narrative and it is this which I think is the fruitful area for liturgical studies: and the question is not 'what' but 'how'.

Narrative theory and the liturgy

It is my hope that the implied readers of this book are already making connections between what I have said about narrative in general and the sort of narratives presented in the liturgy. I have suggested that the role of the liturgy is to insert ourselves into salvation history such that we might appropriate and participate in salvation history in an acute and predetermined fashion and consequently live out our lives as part of that history. Human beings organize their self-understanding narratively: if I ask you to tell me who you are, you are likely to respond with a narrative of the most pertinent aspects of your life connected so as to form a coherent narrative in the context of its telling. The liturgy is where my narrative and God's meet; liturgical authors, like other authors, construct a discourse where aspects of these narratives are set out according to genres, involving characters and plot, and with varying degrees of success or coherence.

The liturgical narrative concerns salvation history, in its entirety or in selected parts; the plot is the way in which the events of salvation history are combined in the texts. As we know, the plot may change according to a church's theological and ecclesiological presuppositions; this is most especially evident in sacramental liturgies, but it is also discernable in the offices and in informal, or non-liturgical worship.

Even without the text in front of us, participation in liturgy can be rather akin to reading. We are presented with the perspective of the authors who select events and ideas and weave them into a narrative, the resultant discourse is the text in which the narrative is presented. These texts will be affected by the inclinations of the author, the criteria of the genre chosen, the selection of the characters to participate in it. The worshippers are not normally the characters in the story, nor actors in a play; as participants we are like readers, responsible for world-making from the narrative presented. It is thus vitally important that those responsible for worship pay attention to the narratives which are presented in the liturgical texts, if it is indeed, as I argue, that the manner of telling and the content of the story of salvation and the way in which we participate in it liturgically which affects how we integrate it into our self-understanding.

A narrative interpretation of liturgical texts

So turning to look at some specific ways in which narrative is used in liturgical texts we can see that there are different levels of narrative intent in different liturgical provision. We might wish to classify these as follows:

overtly narrative – stational liturgies, the liturgical year, Palm Sunday ceremonies

implicitly narrative – eucharistic and initiatory liturgies

non-intentional narrative – the daily offices

Liturgical historians often make use of what might be called para-liturgical texts in which the liturgy is described and explained, such that a text which is implicitly or non-intentionally narrative is made explicitly so using examples drawn from life or from scripture. These explanations are practically never in the form of a theological treatise in technical language, but are illustrative events or stories provided in homilies and commentaries. Thus the liturgical event, which itself contains narrative elements as it takes the participants from point A to point B, as it acts as a transition between stages in life, or simply in the day, has imposed upon it, by a preacher, additional narrative features in the form of explanations. Now the explanation provides a clarification of the plot as it were, it enables the listener to make sense of the sequence of words and

actions in the liturgical event, to provide causal reasons for each
stage. In making these connections the preacher seeks to enable the
listener to join their life experience with the tradition's narratives
in order that they can see themselves as participants in salvation
history. This is most clearly shown in the 'mystagogical catecheses',
the instruction given to baptismal candidates on the liturgy, and
a distinctive feature of this genre is using the story of salvation to
illustrate the participation of the baptismal candidates in it, during
and as a consequence of baptism. In these texts we can identify
the protagonists, the types of stories used, the dominant typology
indicating the preferred theology of baptism, and the manner in
which the candidates participate in the story. The five mystagogical
catecheses from Jerusalem are not the only example but are useful
here for their vivid and compelling narrative.[16] These instructions
were delivered to the newly baptized in the week after Easter by
the bishop of Jerusalem, either by Cyril in the 380s or more likely
by his successor John in the early fifth century. They are one of the
most important sources for the liturgies of baptism and Eucharist
for the post-Constantinian church.

The rite of baptism is explained through the narrative framework
of death and resurrection – that of Christ, and of the candidates
by imitation and participation. Within this overarching narrative
are subplots: the renunciation and adherence is explained in terms
of the flight from Egypt; the immersion as the burial of Christ;
the chrismation by means of the descent of the Holy Spirit upon
Christ at his baptism. In each of these subplots the candidates
imitate the characters in the stories: thus in pre-immersion rituals
they are told that the renunciation of Satan is like the flight of the
Hebrews:

> For when Pharaoh, that most cruel and ruthless tyrant, oppressed
> the free and high-born people of the Hebrews, God sent Moses
> to bring them out of the evil enslavement of the Egyptians. Then
> the door posts were anointed with the blood of the lamb, that the
> destroyer might flee from the houses which had the sign of the

---

[16]There is some dispute about the authorship and date of these *Mystagogical
Catecheses*, although they were undoubtedly preached in Jerusalem at the end of the
fourth or early fifth century. For a discussion of these issues and of the liturgical rite
presupposed by these catecheses see my *Baptismal Liturgy of Jerusalem*.

blood; and the Hebrew people were marvellously delivered. The enemy, however, after their rescue, pursued them and saw the sea marvellously parted for them; nevertheless he went on, following in their footsteps, and was all at once overwhelmed and engulfed in the Red Sea.[17]

This explanation only sets the scene, because the preacher goes on to show how the candidates themselves participate in salvation in a similar way by taking on the role of the Hebrews, just as Christ plays the part of Moses:

There we have Moses sent from God to Egypt; here, Christ sent by His Father into the world; there Moses might lead forth an oppressed people out of Egypt, here that Christ might rescue humanity who are overwhelmed by sin; there the blood of the lamb was the spell against the destroyer, here the blood of the unblemished lamb Jesus Christ is made the charm to scare evil spirits; there the tyrant pursued even to the sea the ancient people, and in like manner this daring and shameless spirit, the author of evil, followed you, even to the very streams of salvation. The tyrant of old was drowned in the sea, and this present one disappears in the saving waters.[18]

The candidates are invited to adopt the position of the Hebrews and to identify their deliverance from a real and pressing enemy in the same way as it is presented in the biblical account of the Exodus.

Attention to the narrative can yield other results in this text too which are of interest in reconstructing the history of baptism. In this text, the candidates' participation in Christ's passion ends at the immersion, where each descent into the water mimics each day in the tomb.

After this (the anointing) you were led by the hand to the holy pool of divine Baptism, as Christ was from the Cross to the tomb before you. And each one was asked if he believes in the name of the Father and of the Son and of the Holy Spirit. And you

---

[17]Cyril (or John) of Jerusalem, *MC* 1.2.
[18]Ibid., 1.3.

agreed to the saving confession, and went down three times into
the water and rose up again and intimated through a symbol the
three day burial of Christ. For just as our Saviour was put in the
heart of the earth for three days and three nights, and so also you
in the first emergence have imitated Christ's first day in the earth
and by the immersion, the night; . . . .[19]

It is not possible, however, to explain the chrismation which
follows the immersion using the same narrative, nor even the
same technique, so now the liturgical action is explained by the
completely different narrative of the baptism of Christ and the
descent of the Spirit. The candidates are to think of themselves as
Christ in the Jordan:

> He also bathed himself in the river Jordan and having imparted
> of the fragrance of his Godhead to the waters, He came up from
> them; and the Holy Ghost in substance lighted upon him, like
> resting upon like. In the same manner to you also, after you
> had come up from the pool of the sacred streams, was given the
> unction, the emblem of that wherewith Christ was anointed, and
> this is the Holy Ghost.[20]

We note also that the narrative now goes backwards in time to
the start of Christ's ministry. This change in dominant typology
indicates a dissonance in the overarching narrative of this baptismal
liturgy which could suggest a recent revision of the rite following
the adoption of liturgical elements from elsewhere which have not
been properly integrated into the narrative.

Looking at a para-liturgical text which contains an overt
narrative provides a useful template with which to turn to look at a
contemporary liturgical text. The main points to be taken from this
example can be summarized as follows:

- There is a specific type of discourse in homiletic and
  catechetical material which is discursive and does not

[19]Ibid., 2.4.
[20]Ibid., 3.1.

just convey information. This type of discourse has as its function the aim of making the listeners identify with and appropriate that which is being said, not simply assent to it.

- The liturgical events of the initiation rite are not listed as events in a chronicle, the audience are not simply told what has happened to them, but an elaborate plot is woven in which they and Christ participate. Events in these parallel narratives are connected together and reasons given for the connection.

- We notice the introduction of a new story line for the chrismation. In homiletic and catechetical material investigating why the preacher has needed to make such a major shift may furnish evidence for newly borrowed, but not integrated, liturgical units.

- We have seen how the major character of the plots is, of course, Christ, but the links between his story and the liturgical events are such that the candidates become characters in the plot too. The identification with and participation in Christ is to be so complete that the candidates may themselves become 'christs' and interpret their own lives through his.[21]

- This text plays with the time frame. Christ's story is not told in chronological order: the passion comes before the baptism. Time is collapsed by the connection between the liturgical events they had experienced a few days ago and the events of Christ's life and of the Exodus. The foundational events are not placed into a historical context but are archetypal events which stand outside time, they are thus immediately available for appropriation in any time.

Bearing this in mind, let us turn to the narrative elements present in contemporary Eucharistic prayers.

---

[21]In *MC* 3.1, through a play on words involving chrism and Christ, the candidates are expressly told that they have become 'christs'.

Eucharistic narratives

Although we would accept that the dominant narrative in the Eucharist is the Last Supper, this is not always the major plotline in the prayer texts. So in traditions which emphasize the Eucharist as commemorative and which may not have fixed forms of Eucharistic prayers, the account of the Supper may well be read with little else. This can be found in the Reformed traditions exemplified by Knox's *Church Order*, and continued in the Church of Scotland's *Book of Common Order* (2005), where the institution narrative is followed by an exhortation to worthy reception and a thanksgiving. At the end of 'The Manner of the Lord's Supper', Knox includes an explanation of why the account of the Last Supper is read:

> And as for the wordes of the Lords Supper, we rehearse them, not because they shulde change the substance of the bread or wine, or that the repetition thereof, with the intent of the sacrificer, shulde make the Sacrament . . . but they are red and pronounced, to teach us how to behave ourselves in that action, and that Christ might witnesse unto our faith, as it were with his own mouth, that he hath ordained these signes to our spirituall use and comfort.[22]

Here Knox indicates that the people's response to the Lord's Supper is to be modelled upon that indicated by Christ and the apostles at the Last Supper and that reading the narrative enables them to play their part when thanks are given, and the bread and wine are distributed.

Similarly, in the book of resources for Baptist worship, *Gathering for Worship*, the account of the Last Supper is to be read from 1 Corinthians 11 and it is separate from the prayer over the bread and wine.[23] In distinction, though, the prayer contains an interpretation

---

[22]*The Liturgy of John Knox received by the Church of Scotland in 1564* (Glasgow: University Press, 1886), pp. 145–6. <http://archive.org/stream/liturgyjohnknox00kn oxuoft#page/146/mode/2up> [accessed 30 March 2012].
[23]Ellis and Blyth, *Gathering for Worship*, pp. 15–16.

of the 1 Corinthians account in which a theological narrative is placed over the foundational narrative indicating a move from story to plot.

In Eucharistic prayers based on the traditional patterns we can note that the narrative in which the Eucharist is situated can start at different points. The preface situates the Eucharistic action within a specific part of salvation history and thereby situates our participation somewhere in it too. Some prayers place us and this particular liturgical event in a cosmic context; thus the prayer encapsulates the power of God in creation, the salvific events of the Old Testament and the incarnation, passion, resurrection of Christ as part of God's ongoing involvement in the world through the power of the Spirit. An elaborate pre-Sanctus listing various types of angelic beings with whom we shall sing the Sanctus places us around the throne of God in heaven. The liturgical action has as its setting not this community in this place in this time, but is beyond time. The characters in the narrative may be the Father, Son and Holy Spirit, the angelic beings, and in some instances patriarchs, prophets, apostles, martyrs, and somewhere, of course, the present worshippers. Our role in this liturgical event is not to play the part of the disciples having a meal with Jesus, but to be witnesses before the throne of God in the heavenly court. In contrast, there are prayers with a purely Christological emphasis where the preface opens with thanksgiving for the incarnation and passion. Here the narrative with which we are surrounded is the historically constrained narrative of the gospels, and the doctrinal 'plot' of the creed. Then again, we also need to note the Western tradition of variable Eucharistic prefaces and the effect they can have on the coherence of the narrative.

As an example, I shall look at one of the Eucharistic prayers provided for the Church of England in *Common Worship: Services and Prayers* (2000) which has a 'default preface' as well as the option of variable prefaces for specific celebrations, in this case I shall select that for the feast of the Ascension. The sort of questions we shall ask of the prayer relate to the presentation of the narrative and how these might affect the 'world-making' of the worshippers.

Common Worship: Eucharistic Prayer B[24]

Default preface

Father, we give you thanks and
    praise
through your beloved Son Jesus
    Christ, your living Word,
through whom you have created all
    things;
who was sent by you in your great
    goodness to be our Saviour.

By the power of the Holy Spirit he
    took flesh;
as your Son, born of the blessed
    Virgin,
he lived on earth and went about
    among us;
he opened wide his arms for us on
    the cross;
he put an end to death by dying for
    us;
and revealed the resurrection by
    rising to new life;
so he fulfilled your will and won for
    you a holy people.

Therefore with angels and
    archangels,
and with all the company of heaven,
we proclaim your great and glorious
    name,
for ever praising you and saying:

Ascension Day preface

It is indeed right and good,
our duty and our joy,
always and everywhere to give
    you thanks,
holy Father, almighty and
    eternal God,
through Jesus Christ the King
    of glory.
Born of a woman,
he came to the rescue of our
    human race.
Dying for us,
he trampled death and
    conquered sin.
By the glory of his resurrection
he opened the way to life
    eternal
and by his ascension,
gave us the sure hope
that where he is we may also
    be.
Therefore the universe resounds
    with Easter joy
and with choirs of angels we
    sing for ever to your praise:

Holy, holy, holy Lord,
God of power and might,
heaven and earth are full of your glory.
Hosanna in the highest.
[Blessed is he who comes in the name of the Lord.
Hosanna in the highest.]

---

[24]CW, Order One: Eucharistic Prayer B, pp. 188–90 with the Extended Preface for
Ascension, p. 319.

Lord, you are holy indeed, the source of all holiness;
grant that by the power of your Holy Spirit,
and according to your holy will,
these gifts of bread and wine
may be to us the body and blood of our Lord Jesus Christ;

who, in the same night that he was betrayed,
took bread and gave you thanks;
he broke it and gave it to his disciples, saying:
Take, eat; this is my body which is given for you;
do this in remembrance of me.

In the same way, after supper
he took the cup and gave you thanks;
he gave it to them, saying:
Drink this, all of you;
this is my blood of the new covenant,
which is shed for you and for many for the forgiveness of sins.
Do this, as often as you drink it,
in remembrance of me.

One of these four acclamations is used

[Great is the mystery of faith:]	[Praise to you, Lord Jesus:]	[Christ is the bread of life:]	[Jesus Christ is Lord:]
Christ has died: Christ is risen: Christ will come again.	Dying you destroyed our death, rising you restored our life: Lord Jesus, come in glory.	When we eat this bread and drink this cup, we proclaim your death, Lord Jesus, until you come in glory.	Lord, by your cross and resurrection you have set us free. You are the Saviour of the world.

And so, Father, calling to mind his death on the cross,
his perfect sacrifice made once for the sins of the whole world;
rejoicing in his mighty resurrection and glorious ascension,
and looking for his coming in glory,
we celebrate this memorial of our redemption.
As we offer you this our sacrifice of praise and thanksgiving,
we bring before you this bread and this cup

and we thank you for counting us worthy
to stand in your presence and serve you.

Send the Holy Spirit on your people
and gather into one in your kingdom
all who share this one bread and one cup,
so that we, in the company of [N and] all the saints,
may praise and glorify you for ever,
through Jesus Christ our Lord;

by whom, and with whom, and in whom,
in the unity of the Holy Spirit,
all honour and glory be yours, almighty Father,
for ever and ever.
Amen.

With the almost exclusive attention on Christ's saving acts this
prayer has a distinctive Christological emphasis. The default preface
hints at the eternal coexistence of the Son, cocreating with the Father,
but the sequence of events begins with the annunciation and skips
through the birth, life, death and resurrection, before returning us
to the cosmic level with the angelic song. These are told as a story,
a series of events with, as yet, no indication of cause, and therefore
no plot. What is the causal relationship between the statements in
this preface? We might ask why these particular events have been
chosen and what do they demonstrate? They obviously do have a
purpose because we are then told that because of them we should
praise God with the angels in the Sanctus.

By selecting a variable preface, it is possible to show how changes
in telling the story and the presence of explicit causal relations affect
how the recipients might interpret the narrative. Here the story
again begins with Christ, there is no hint of anything before the
birth which, because of a gap in the narrative, has not necessarily
occurred due to the intervention of the Holy Spirit. However, the
variable preface does provide an explanation for every event:

he was born – that we might be saved
he died – and conquered sin
he rose – and opened for us eternal life
he ascended – so we can hope to ascend to heaven too (by
implication)

In these examples we can see how the events are linked so that they demonstrate the work of salvation, a plot is developed. According to this preface, these named things and our expressed desire to 'be where [Christ] is' cause us to inevitably praise God with the angels.

When they reach the Sanctus, worshippers who have heard the default prayer and those who have heard the variable preface are in quite different places vis-à-vis the story of salvation. The former are being asked to take on trust that there is a relationship between the narrative of Christ's life and work and them; the latter have a much better chance of linking the events to themselves and their salvation. Note that in both, the prayer makes assumptions about the temporal and spatial connection of the immediate congregation and the company of heaven: there is little to suggest that they are to believe themselves standing before the heavenly throne until the Sanctus implies it. The temporal and spatial emphasis is initially located in Christ's earthly ministry, that is in Palestine in the first century.

Narratives have a pace and that is usually determined by the amount of space an event is given in the telling of it: we have seen so far that the thirty years of Christ's earthly ministry have been compressed into four or five lines, but the account of the Last Supper invariably slows down the narrative as we focus upon the events during one evening meal. Before that though, the epiclesis of the Holy Spirit placed before the institution narrative indicates a possible lack of coherence in the discourse: we are asked to believe that the bread and wine might be the body and blood of Christ, with the help of the Holy Spirit, but as yet we have no idea why we might want them to be. The subsequent presentation of the events of the Supper do explain this, so that by the end of the prayer we have the means to link the ideas together. Not all narratives move in chronological order and where there is disorder then the recipient must work harder to reorganize them in her mind so that the story and the plot make sense. By the end of this section, the recipients know what happened at the supper table, they know that Christ made a connection between bread and his body, wine and his blood, that they are to remind themselves of this when they eat bread and drink wine, and that this is what we are doing by consuming the bread and wine at that Eucharist. As we read the prayer, though, we find that the last point is made first.

So far the recipients are aware that consuming bread and wine is in obedience to Christ's command, but the text has not provided any clues as to how or why this might be related to their own salvation and to salvation history. The acclamations and anamnesis which follow make a more explicit connection between what we are doing here and Christ's salvific work on the cross – his death is for our sins, his resurrection, ascension and return are all part of the saving action. The events mentioned in the anamnesis are mostly in the past, but reference is made also to the present and the future – Christ died, rose and ascended in the past; we stand before God and serve him now; and Christ will come in the future. The chronology is implied in the anamnesis more than in the acclamations. Because of the gaps in the narrative of the default preface the recipients will have a greater need of the explanatory sections of the anamnesis than those receiving the Ascension Day preface. The latter have already heard that the reason for Christ's death is sin, whereas this is the first time it has been mentioned in the default prayer.

A story involves characters. The first 'character' is the Father who is the one to receive our thanks and praise, but has little clear role apart from that. Christ enacts the principal events of the narrative and only in the default preface is his relationship to the Father stated – he is Son and Word – but nothing is said to this effect in the Ascension Day preface. The Holy Spirit, who in the past caused the Son to take flesh, now enables us to relate the Eucharistic elements to Christ's body and blood and who, at an indeterminate time now or in the future, will gather us into the kingdom. This summary of the characters shows that although the prayer is Christological in emphasis, Christ's role is somewhat static as the one to whom the events happened, but the Holy Spirit has a more dynamic role over a longer timeframe; by contrast, the Father is almost entirely passive.

Stepping back from the content of the text to enquire about how the narrative functions a series of questions need to be asked. Who is the recipient of this narrative? Is it us or is it God? Is there a real and/or implied author? Who is the real and/or implied narrator? Who are the real and/or implied recipients? There are sufficient narrative elements in this Eucharistic prayer to call it such, but if narrative is related by a narrator to a narratee, and at another level an author communicates to a reader, who takes on these roles in the prayer? In performance the prayer is predominantly spoken by the priest, but no one would mistake him for the author. There is a preference for 'we' over 'I', but this is not the 'Royal We' which really means 'I', but a 'we' of the assembly.[25] By implication the events are narrated by the assembly, but they are also narrated to the assembly, as such it really does function as one of the stories we tell ourselves about ourselves in order to form and establish identity.

The prayer, though, is addressed to God, specifically to the Father. He is asked to recall various events and to act in sending the Holy Spirit. We tell him the story and draw out certain inferences that make sense of the recalled events. So at the level of the narrative, the narrattee is God the Father. The prayer was composed for use in the Church of England and therefore there is already an implied recipient, that is Anglicans in England, but the text may make further assumptions about these recipients based on notions of Christian maturity, linguistic and conceptual abilities, and that those hearing the prayer will indeed be those who receive the bread and wine at the conclusion of the prayer. These assumptions may or may not be borne out when the prayer is used on a Sunday morning with an actual congregation, and it is only at this point that the real recipient comes into focus. It is these real recipients who will be required to make sense of the narrative using whatever information the prayer provides and any techniques they have acquired in worship and as consumers of other narratives.

What about notions of authorship displayed in the text? Just as much as the text proposes an implied reader, it also proposes an implied author. An assembly which uses this prayer will claim it as their own, they will use the words as if they were their own words. Thus the implied author of the prayer is each congregation which uses it, hence the difficult task of the real authors on the liturgical committees.

Conclusion

The use of narrative theory can take us into some rich pastures for liturgical research as we explore roles in the narrative and how the

---

[25]This observation raises an interesting point in relation to concelebration where there is the risk that the 'we' of the prayer becomes 'we the priests' rather than 'we the assembly'.

story of salvation is plotted in a variety of liturgical texts. But on a practical and pastoral level, if Christians are formed by the stories we tell about ourselves, then the coherence of the liturgical narrative is of fundamental importance. What we include and exclude may be determined by the context of the narrating – thus at Christmas we naturally expect something to be said about the incarnation and, at the very least, the story of the nativity to be told. It may not be necessary to include everything all the time, but attending to whether the whole story is being told throughout a cycle of liturgies may be illuminating. Liturgical authors may well want to consider whether our liturgical narratives have gaps which are just too great for the community to fill adequately from their own resources and thus it is not simply that the worshippers may not know the story, it is also that the story can sometimes be presented in a way which eludes comprehension.

5

Intertextuality

The recognition of other texts in a liturgical text by worshippers is not an uncommon experience as, for example, when they encounter biblical passages which may have been read in full at some stage during the cycle of lections. The reuse might be a quotation, allusion, paraphrase or just the barest hint, and each of these potentially allow the worshipper to bring the other texts into the interpretation of the liturgical text they are reading or hearing. The ability to make a connection is, to a great extent, dependent upon the competency of the worshipper, their familiarity with scripture and with the forms and structures of liturgical texts, and these are matters over which the author has no control. We have already noted the limitations on creativity for liturgical authors; they are constrained to a large degree by conventions and expectations, by genre and by the formula and themes of a particular prayer type. Additionally, though, they are influenced by other prayer texts – liturgical authors are first worshippers – that is, in the process of liturgical composition, they are inevitably bound to draw upon the acts of worship in which they have participated to provide the language and structure of the new texts.

Intertextuality refers to the presence of texts within texts and its study may provide us with a means to investigate the processes of selection and incorporation of texts and how they work upon the reader (worshipper) to influence their meaning-making. Intertextuality is the phenomenon of inserting and identifying textual material from elsewhere, the intertext is that which is inserted. In what follows we shall more closely define these terms and then employ them in our discussion of some particular examples of liturgical intertextuality. From liturgical historical studies we

shall return to the anaphora of Serapion and the curious presence of
an apparent allusion to the *Didache*; from familiar liturgical texts
we shall examine the juxtaposition of unrelated biblical texts in
the Sanctus–Benedictus unit of the Eucharistic prayer, an opaque
allusion in a post-communion prayer and the 'collage' of biblical
passages at the start of the Burial Service in the Book of Common
Prayer.

Intertextuality and the intertext

There are two principal approaches to intertextuality. The first,
proposed by Julia Kristeva and Roland Barthes, considers all texts
to be intertextual, as Barthes wrote:

> any text is an intertext; other texts are present in it, at varying
> levels, in more or less recognisable forms: the texts of the
> previous and surrounding cultures. Any text is a new tissue
> of past citations. . . . Intertextuality, the condition of any text
> whatsoever, cannot, of course, be reduced to a problem of
> sources and influences; the intertext is a field of anonymous
> formulae whose origin can scarcely ever be located . . .[1]

The second uses intertextuality in a more limited way to refer to
deliberate acts of borrowing by authors. Although nuanced in
different ways this is the perspective of Michael Riffaterre and
Gérard Genette,[2] and it is more useful for liturgical texts because of
the more limited corpus from which liturgcal intertexts are drawn.
In this model the presence of an intertext is a purposed authorial act
in which the intention is that the reader will make the connection
and, in doing so, bring an extra dimension to the meaning they
derive from the text.

Focusing on the intertext itself, rather than intertextuality as a
literary phenomenon, we need first to clarify its role in the text.

---

[1]Roland Barthes, 'The Theory of the Text', in Robert Young (ed.), *Untying the Text:
A Post Structuralist Reader* (London: Routledge and Keegan Paul, 1981) p. 39. See
also the discussion of Barthes in Graham Allen, *Intertextuality* (London and New
York: Routledge, 2000), chapter 2.
[2]See Allen, *Intertextuality*, chapter 3.

Heinrich Plett offered a simple distinction of the intertext as 'a text *between* other texts'.[3] At first the reader encounters the text which is being read; then encounters the intertext, a quotation or other allusion, etc.; and then, through the intertext, encounters the source text. Each of these texts plays a different role: the text before one has structural boundaries and a coherent arrangement of its content into a meaningful whole; the intertext, though, is only the partial representation of the source text. The intertext appears as an alien element in the text, it points beyond itself and to be meaningful requires both the text and an awareness of the source text. The source, or 'pre-text' as Plett designates it, is commonly hidden from view, it is only partially present and its meaningfulness may be of limited relevance in the interpretation of the text being read. How relevant it is depends on the function of the intertext and the author's intentions.

Further, Plett distinguished three levels of quotation: authoritative, erudite and ornamental.[4] The former would immediately appear to relate to the liturgical context where quotation is a 'ritualized' act from a source whose authority is unquestioned, that is the Bible. The 'erudite' quotation permits disagreement, and thus is unlikely to be proffered in a worship context. And 'ornamental' quotations which 'serve as decorative embellishments added to the substance of the text' are quite likely to appear in some liturgical texts and these, he argues, may be removed without harm to the context.[5]

Readers will become alert to quotations by devices such as punctuation marks or indentation; these 'textual signs' immediately alert the reader to the presence of an intertext, they cause a temporary hiatus in the flow of the text as the reader considers the function of the intertext in relation to the text.[6] The information to enable the reader to connect with the source text may often be provided following the conventions of references or footnotes, as it

---

[3]Heinrich F. Plett, 'Intertextualities', idem. (ed.), *Intertextuality, Research in Text Theory* vol. 15 (Berlin: De Gruyter, 1991), p. 5.

[4]Ibid., p. 13.

[5]Ibid., pp. 13–14.

[6]Worton and Still refer to quotations as a 'blocking mechanism which (temporarily at least) restricts the readers free, aleatory intertextual reading of the text': Michael Worton and Judith Still, 'Introduction', idem., *Intertextuality: Theories and Practice* (Manchester: Manchester University Press, 1990), p. 10.

is in this book. A very obvious paraphrase may work in a similar way. A collection of quotations from a variety of sources juxtaposed with each other, to form what has been called a 'collage', will also make itself known to the reader by similar textual signs; however, now the intertexts collude with each other to create meaning in the context of the text, but with less attachment to their source texts. The meaning-making task of the reader is to fill in the gaps between them, to create connections where there may be none in and between the source texts and here the author demands considerably more work from the reader than in other forms of intertextuality.

But where the intertext is only an allusion, then the reader has a choice whether to recognize it, it usually being without any textual signs, and then to recall the source text in order to begin to discern the author's meaning. Of course the reader may choose not to do this work, or indeed she may not even recognize an allusion at all, and this is a risk the author must take. Furthermore as Riffaterre has said,

> we must distinguish between the actual knowledge of the form and content of that intertext and a mere awareness that such an intertext exists and can eventually be found somewhere. This awareness in itself may be enough to make readers experience the text's literariness. They can do so because they perceive that something is missing from the text: gaps that need to be filled, references to an as yet unknown referent, references whose successive occurrences map out, as it were, the outline of the intertext still to be discovered.[7]

The allusion has only the potential to disrupt the flow of reading, and only potentially be available for adding meaning to the text, whether it does or not is largely dependent upon the clues provided by the author and the 'competence' of the reader; an allusion may be passed over without recognition or comment, such is the way in which it is embedded in the text.

The deployment of an intertext follows the 'logic' of the text in which it is placed and may have little relation to the

---

[7]Michael Riffaterre, 'Compulsory Reader Response: The Intertextual Drive', in Worton and Still, *Intertextuality*, pp. 56–7.

original context. This has the effect of erasing the contextual distinctions of the source text, one of which is, of course, the time of its composition. Intertextuality presumes that all texts exist simultaneously and can be related to any other text whatsoever.[8] The author is under no requirement to arrange material chronologically, for example, and this we can clearly see in the use of biblical quotations and allusions in liturgical texts which are not arranged according to the sequence of biblical books nor even to a perceived biblical chronology, but rather according to the theological preferences of the author.

As Riffaterre said in the quotation above, intertextuality makes us aware of the 'literariness' of a text; texts are woven from other texts and not from prior speech. They are woven from source texts available to the author and presumed to be also available to the reader, if not already known to her. Texts create meaning through the connections between texts. Canonical texts, traditionally in English Shakespeare, the King James Bible and the Book of Common Prayer, are presumed to be widely available in a given cultural context forming part of the shared textual culture so that they need not be actively recalled by the author or reader when writing or reading. These source texts have moved out of the textual boundaries into general language, used without regard to their original context but in relation to numerous other instances of their being cited or alluded to. As we shall explore below on the Sanctus and Benedictus, even an obvious intertext may not be used in relation to its meaning in the source text but to an interpretation placed upon it by other intermediary texts.

A consideration of intertextuality forces us to place the interpretation of a text firmly in the hands, or mind, of the reader. The author is unable to control the range of possible connections which a reader may bring to her text once an intertext is recognized. Although the author may have a clear referent in mind, the reader is free to use whatever resources she has available in her past reading. There is no limit to the possibilities for the generation of meaning as an infinite 'network of textual relations'[9] are brought to bear.

---

[8]Plett, 'Intertextualities', p. 25. He refers to this as the synchronic view of intertextuality.

[9]Allen, *Intertextuality*, p. 1.

Intertextuality and liturgical texts

The remainder of this chapter will explore how obvious intertexts in liturgical texts may function and may be interpreted. Clearly scripture provides the primary source text, but it is used in quite different ways to different effect in each liturgical text; an intertext may indicate itself in overt or subtle ways, and there is no absolute requirement for faithfulness to the source text. Worshippers may, and certainly do, bring their own 'network of textual relations' to the interpretative process in ways which might surprise the authors of liturgical texts. Attention to the way texts embed other texts has uses for liturgical historical studies by moving away from a simple source critical approach to consider how meaning is created in the gaps between the text and the source text, rather than simply identifying a specific source text. It also offers important insights into the reception of contemporary liturgical texts which exhibit different types of intertext, especially in secular cultures where biblical literacy is low.

An apparent quotation in Serapion's anaphora

A quotation is an explicit intertextual element, in modern printed texts it will identify itself by quotation marks and in some genres by a footnote reference. The reader may also be alerted to the presence of an intertext by a change of literary style and by an obvious disruption to an anticipated sequence of words or ideas. Just such an intertext is present in the anaphora of Serapion, where the institution narrative is disrupted by a quotation from the *Didache*, a text dated to the latter parts of the first century and presumed to be Syrian.[10] The sacramentary of Serapion is preserved in a single manuscript, catalogued as MS Lavra 149, in which the text is presented without punctuation, and certainly without footnotes! Maxwell Johnson in preparing his greek text of the sacramentary from the manuscript noted the difficulty of indicating scriptural intertexts, 'Because

---

[10]See Thomas O'Loughlin, *The Didache: A Window on the Earliest Christians* (London: SPCK, 2010), pp. 26–7.

it is often difficult to tell if certain words or phrases are actually intended to be biblical allusions or are merely part of the Church's general liturgical and theological vocabulary . . . it is impossible to be completely accurate' in providing footnotes.[11] The particular intertext that we shall investigate, however, is a quotation from a non-scriptural source embedded in the institution narrative:

> To you we offer this bread, the likeness of the body of the only-begotten. This bread is the likeness of the holy body. For the Lord Jesus Christ, in the night when he was handed over, took bread, broke it, and gave it to his disciples, saying: Take and eat, this is my body which is broken for you for the forgiveness of sins. Therefore, we also offered the bread making the likeness of the death. And we implore you through this sacrifice, God of truth: be reconciled to us all and be merciful. *And as this bread (artos) was scattered over the mountains and, when it was gathered together, became one, so also gather your holy church out of every nation and every region and every city and village and house and make one living catholic church.* And we also offered the cup, the likeness of blood. For the Lord Jesus Christ, taking a cup after supper, said to the disciples: Take, drink, this is the new covenant, which is my blood poured out for you for the forgiveness of sins. Therefore, we also offered the cup presenting the likeness of the blood.[12]

Didache 9.4 reads:

> Just as this broken *(klasma)* [loaf] was scattered over the hills [as grain], and, having been gathered together became one; in like fashion, may your church be gathered together from the ends of the earth into your kingdom.[13]

There are, it must be noted, some minor changes in the rendering by Serapion. He substitutes *klasma*, a 'broken thing', which in the context of the *Didache* and this prayer can only be a loaf or bread,

[11]Johnson, *Sarapion*, p. 45.
[12]Ibid., p. 49. Emphasis mine.
[13]Aaron Milavec, *The Didache: Faith, Hope, and Life of the Earliest Christian Communities, 50–70 C.E.* (Mahwah, NJ: Newman Press, 2003), p. 33.

with *artos*, explicitly 'bread'. There are minor grammatical changes which do not affect the sense and which can be explained by the need to harmonize the tenses in the target text. At the end Serapion asks that the gathering is into 'one church' (*ekklesia*), and not into 'the kingdom' (*basileia*). The differences are not sufficient to indicate that Serapion was simply introducing a stock phrase from a reserve of Eucharistic themes, but rather that he was familiar with the *Didache* and that this is an explicit intertext. Of more interest, though, is why he inserted this quotation at this particular place in the anaphora and what that might tell us about his intended worshippers.

Clearly, there has been much debate over the presence of this sentence in the anaphora, particularly as it divides the two parts of the institution narrative. Historians of the liturgy have attempted a source critical analysis to reveal what model of the institution narrative Serapion might have had, or they have looked for authorial intention (that is, his theological and ecclesiological imperatives) to explain its presence. Source criticism led Wobbermin and Wordsworth to state that Serapion was familiar with the *Didache*, and Bouyer and Mazza that Serapion was influenced either by *Apostolic Constitutions* 7.25 or that they both shared a common source.[14] As for authorial intention, Capelle suggested that Serapion was making an innovative theological point about the return of Arians to the catholic church, but makes no comment on the very presence of the quotation.[15] And, Dix considered that,

> The unsuitability of describing the corn from which the eucharistic bread has been made as having been 'scattered on the tops of the mountains' among the mud flats of the Nile delta makes it plain that this is not an authentic product of the native tradition of the prayer at Thmuis, but a rather unimaginative *literary* quotation.[16]

---

[14]These views are summarized by Johnson (*Sarapion*, p. 224). However, *Apostolic Constitutions* 7.25 interpolates a version of *Didache* 9.4 into a very different type of institution narrative and, additionally, the accepted date of compilation is 380 by which time Serapion was clearly no longer alive.

[15]See Johnson, *Sarapion*, p. 224.

[16]Gregory Dix, *The Shape of the Liturgy* (2nd ed. repr. London: Continuum, 2001[1945]), p. 167 (his italics).

Source criticism has enabled the identification of the source text and one possible intermediary text, but can tell us nothing about why Serapion might have included it; the theological interpretation may provide a motive for its inclusion, although it cannot explain why Serapion should choose to insert this particular statement at this particular point in the anaphora. Dix did at least note that the presence of *Didache* 9.4 was incongruous and, risking an anachronism, he did identify an intertext because of the shift in tone and context, which quite frankly does render it a rather ludicrous insertion. It is, of course, impossible to recover Serapion's intentions at the point of composition, indeed associating the bread of the Last Supper with the bread of the *Didache* may have been entirely unconscious.[17]

Intertexts may be categorized as purposed, playful and ornamental. It would be unusual for a liturgical author to insert a 'playful' intertext into a liturgical text, that is an intertext which referred to a text which did not exist, a parody. With a playful intertext, the reader is sent on a wild goose chase to identify the intertext which, as it does not exist, leads her back to the text itself. As we can identify the source of this intertext, clearly Serapion was not being playful. An author may insert an intertext for ornamental reasons, that is it does not contribute to the generation of meaning but adds aesthetic value; is this intertext then simply a rhetorical flourish? In such instances the reader is not expected to derive meaning from it, but this too seems unlikely because of the changes which Serapion has made to harmonize the intertext with his anaphora. This leads us to conclude that Serapion deliberately inserted this intertext, because it served his own meaning-making purposes and that he must have expected it to be meaningful to his congregation.

The quotation may also serve to limit the range of meanings available in the text. In the context of Serapion's anaphora, the bread which they are about to consume in the Eucharist is not likened to just any bread such as they may have at their meal, but first with the manna by which God preserved the Hebrews in the desert, and then with the body of Christ. These further allusions serve to illustrate God's desire to unite all people to himself through the covenant

---

[17]If so, then one has to argue that the themes were part of a more widespread Eucharistic theology, but as there is only one other later example of incorporating it into an anaphora (in a quite different way), the evidence for that is weak.

and then through the death and resurrection of Christ. *Didache*
9.4 provides an interpretation of the Eucharist which is divorced
from the narratives of the Last Supper and thus appears to open a
door on a fresh interpretation, but no sooner is that door opened
than the import of the quotation closes off all other avenues of
interpretation. In this instance it is not necessary for the worshipper
to identify the source of the quotation, indeed in its original context
it would only clarify the possibility of interpreting the Eucharist
without explicit regard to the Last Supper and therefore adds
nothing; to the scholar, however, the presence of this text raises all
sorts of questions about the author's intentions, about the literary
context of his community – did they know and read the *Didache*, or
was it mediated to Serapion via another text – and what implications
it might have for Serapion's Eucharistic theology.

Modern readers using critical editions are confronted by the
intertext: Johnson at least does not insert marks into the Greek
or English text, but he does provide a reference in the greek text;[18]
others have been less diligent. The manuscript (MS Lavra 149) bears
no punctuation of any kind and the insertion of full stops, commas,
colons and semicolons is itself a form of interpretation. The
contemporary reader has no choice but to recognize the intertext
and return to the *Didache* to reflect upon how this source text might
help us make sense of the whole anaphora, or just the institution
narrative. If, for example, one looked up a commentary on *Didache*
9.4, such as Milavec's comprehensive work, one would be thrown
back to first-century Jewish eating customs;[19] however, bringing this
to the interpretation of Serapion's fourth-century Egyptian context
would probably be misleading.

A worshipper in Thmuis, c. 350, might have noted the incongruity
of the statement, either because it disrupted the flow of the institution
narrative or because of the oddness of the mountain imagery, but
only if the *Didache* had a place in the communal memory, by being
read in church or used in catechesis, could he bring the two texts
together to create or discover the meaning through the interplay
between them.[20] Without knowledge of the source text, the intertext

---

[18]Johnson, *Sarapion*, p. 48 n. 16.

[19]Milavec, *Didache*, pp. 371–3.

[20]Wobbermin did indeed argue that the Egyptian church was familiar with the
Didache and that *Didache* 9.4 was a common feature of the Greek liturgy. See ibid.,
Altchristliche liturgische Stücke, pp. 25–6.

can only function at the surface of the text, it cannot contribute to
any further generation of meaning and may simply be regarded as
ornamental. Serapion would have been reliant upon his readers/
worshippers to 'get' the intertext in order to make sense of his
prayer; this means that either the *Didache* was a familiar text to the
congregation, or that the scholarly analysis of ancient texts causes
us to seek meaning and purpose where none can be found.

The juxtaposition of biblical quotations in the Eucharistic prayer

Eucharistic prayers in the classical tradition, like that attributed to
John Chrysostom or the Roman Canon and their contemporary
imitators, contain what purport to be direct quotations from other
texts, as well as less detectable allusions. The most obvious borrowed
elements common to all these prayers are the quotation of Isaiah
6 in the Sanctus and the paraphrases of the institution narratives
from the gospels and I Corinthians. These borrowings are usually
indicated in the printed text by quotation marks or indentation and
thus the reader (worshipper or priest) is forced to recognize them as
distinct from the rest of the prayer. Hidden in the prayer might be
less obvious allusions either to scripture or even to other liturgical
texts, for example Eucharistic Prayer 2 in the *Roman Missal* is
based on the anaphora of the *Apostolic Tradition*.

A worshipper may make the connection between intentional
intertexts and some unintended referents in their own cultural
context at any time, and this challenges notions of the stability of
meaning contained in a liturgical text. The liturgical text cannot
contain a fixed interpretation which, through the application of
approved methods, will lead the worshipper to appropriate the
authorized meaning whatever the author intended. Once the text
is in the world it may cause interpretations by worshippers in
light of all and any other text which they have ever read, however
inappropriate.[21] The author may indicate to the reader a limitation
of the other texts which can be brought to the interpretation of

---

[21]For example, interpretation of the traditional reference to the 'devil' in contemporary baptismal liturgies may well be hampered by a particular genre of popular
literature and film.

the target text by overtly directing the reader to the source of the intertext by quotation marks and/or footnotes.

Such directions provide the worshipper with a shortcut to the source text so that, it is presumed, once they are familiar with this they can bring to their interpretation the whole context of the source text. This one assumes is what happens with scriptural quotations: if a worshipper has heard Isaiah 6 or Revelation 4 read as one of the lections, they should be able to connect the singing of the Sanctus in that particular act of worship to the song of the archangels around the throne of God and in doing so they bridge time by connecting the historical context of the book of Isaiah with the present, and also transcend time by connecting the present with the eternal praise of God. A biblical scholar specializing in the book of Isaiah will bring to the Eucharistic Sanctus a considerably more detailed understanding, and will relate Isaiah 6 to yet other biblical and scholarly texts and therefore generate meanings which, although they may be further removed from the Eucharistic Sanctus, are nevertheless legitimately generated by the intertext. And, conversely, the worshipper who is unaware that the Eucharistic Sanctus is from Isaiah 6, will be restricted to its use in the Eucharist only, or, perhaps by attending only to the literal level, they will bring to their interpretation all occurrences of 'Holy, holy, holy' in the hymnal.

In many Eucharistic prayers, the Sanctus is juxtaposed with the Benedictus: 'Blessed is he who comes in the name of the Lord, Hosanna in the Highest'. This, again, is an intertext and we are invited by the liturgical author to interpret the Sanctus in light of this juxtaposed text, to anachronistically interpret an Old Testament passage in light of a New Testament passage, and by a ritual signing with the cross during the Benedictus to relate the text to Christ. The juxtaposition of these two intertexts creates a mystery for the worshipper to unravel. Neither the choice nor their juxtaposition are explained; the ambiguity challenges the worshipper to find the meaning.

Bryan Spinks's comprehensive study of the Sanctus in the Eucharistic prayer, charting its liturgical use from Jewish worship to contemporary liturgical revisions, identifies the biblical and liturgical sources for the form of the Sanctus and the manner in which it has been incorporated into the prayer.[22] He has noted

---

[22]Bryan Spinks, *The Sanctus in the Eucharistic Prayer* (Cambridge: Cambridge University Press, 1991).

that the primary reason for its inclusion is to express the unity of heaven and earth, the whole created order – visible and invisible – in the praise of God, but that not all prayers introduce this element in a manner which would enable the congregation to so situate themselves. Thus, 'Some general theology about heavenly worship, or the weight of tradition, or musical considerations should not be an excuse for simply inserting the Sanctus; it ought to have a logical doxological context.'[23] Where such a context is lacking, by omitting reference to heavenly beings or the worship of the Church, the worshipper is expected to bring to their interpretation of the prayer a prior knowledge of the source text; however, where the context is provided the worshipper is given the option to simply take the surface meaning of the Eucharistic prayer. This can be easily illustrated by comparing the different ways in which the Sanctus is introduced in *Common Worship*'s Eucharistic prayers where the default prefaces are used. Prayers A, B, C have:

Therefore with angels and archangels,
and with all the company of heaven,
we proclaim your great and glorious name,
for ever praising you and saying:[24]

But Prayer F provides:

As we watch for the signs of your kingdom on earth,
we echo the song of the angels in heaven,
evermore praising you and saying:[25]

However, prayers A and B may replace the entire preface from the end of the dialogue until the Sanctus with variable prefaces which tend to emphasize Christological themes, and these may not provide the necessary clues to enable appropriation of the Sanctus without knowledge of the pre-texts.[26]

In performance the Sanctus and Benedictus form an inseparable unit, however attention to intertextuality invites us to be aware

---

[23]Ibid., p. 197.
[24]*CW*, pp. 184–93.
[25]Ibid., p. 198.
[26]See the Extended Preface for Ascension quoted in the previous chapter.

that the Benedictus is a quotation from Matthew 21.9, which itself quotes Psalm 118.26. Elsewhere I have investigated the origins of the Benedictus in the Eucharistic prayer and suggested that the idea is based on the Jewish *Quedushah*, in which the Sanctus was followed by a 'Blessed be' acclamation from Ezekiel 3.2, but that the whole was christianized by the insertion of a 'Blessed be' statement with clear Christological associations that was already in use for Palm Sunday processions.[27] In contemporary performance the Christological association of the Benedictus alone is ritualized by a signing with the cross here, and not with the Sanctus. If, during the Sanctus, the scripturally literate worshipper identifies the context of the source text and then subsequently that of the Benedictus, the incongruence of their juxtaposition should force her to undertake further interpretative work, which overfamiliarity almost certainly hinders. The intertextual elements combine to generate a meaning which is not obvious from the immediate context in which they are placed, and certainly not from the juxtaposition of the two quotations; the worshipper will require more than scripture to work out what is going on and why these texts are juxtaposed.

Spinks noted that the 'Holy, Holy Holy' was used as a hymn to God as Trinity as early as the second century on the evidence of the apocryphal text, the *Ascension of Isaiah* 8.17–18,[28] although subsequent evidence until the late fourth century is scant. Theodore of Mopsoestia in *Homily* 16 is explicit about this interpretation:

> It is necessary, therefore, that the priest also should, after having mentioned in the service the Father, the Son and the Holy Spirit, say: 'Praise and adoration are offered by all the creatures to Divine nature.' He makes mention also of the seraphim, as they are found in the Divine Book singing the praise which all of us who are present sing loudly in the Divine song which all of us recite, along with the invisible hosts, in order to serve God.[29]

---

[27]See my, 'The Origins of the Anaphoral Benedictus', *JTS* 60 (2009), pp. 193–211.
[28]Spinks, *Sanctus*, p. 52.
[29]Theodore of Mopsuestia, *Homily* 16: A. Mingana, *Commentary of Theodore of Mopsuestia on the Lord's Prayer and on the Sacraments of Baptism and the Eucharist*, Woodbrooke Studies 6 (Cambridge: Heffer, 1933), p. 101.

Similar ideas are found in Narsai's homilies as well.[30] The addition of the Benedictus in the late fourth or early fifth century is related to the doctrinal debate about the Trinity and the divinity of Christ. The Benedictus asks the worshipper to connect the thrice-holy God, Trinity of Father, Son and Spirit, with Jesus Christ as the 'one who comes in the name of the Lord' and indeed is the second Person of the Trinity. Such a doctrinal interpretation of these intertexts is confirmed, ironically, by prayers which seem to address the Sanctus to Christ.

Thus, the scripturally literate worshipper is led on a false trail by these intertexts: if she brings to the Sanctus the context of Isaiah 6 and Revelation 4, then the text will retain coherence as sharing in the hymn of praise to God with the heavenly host. When, however, she is next confronted by the Benedictus, recourse to Psalm 118 and Matthew 21 will be of little help in deriving meaning from the juxtaposition of these two intertexts. If, however, the source text is not scripture but varied doctrinal writings and homiletic material of the period when these elements were introduced, then the contextualization expressed in the list of heavenly beings who share in this hymn is highly misleading. The juxtaposition of these two apparently unrelated intertexts can only be understood in relation to orthodox Trinitarian and Christological statements of the fourth century.

A biblical allusion in a collect

An intertext can be identified where the language departs from what is expected in its surroundings and where it becomes apparent that there is a logical gap in the narrative, of ideas or story, or any kind of disjunction. If these alert the reader to an implicit intertext, their understanding of the text will be suspended or limited until they are able to identify the intertext and join its meaning with the target text. An interesting case is provided by a post-communion collect which first made its appearance in the *Alternative Service Book* (1980), and has been retained in *Common Worship* because it has become a valued and much-used liturgical text.

---

[30]Narsai, *Homily* 17. R. H. Connolly, *The Liturgical Homilies of Narsai*, Texts and Studies 8 (Cambridge: Cambridge University Press, 1909), pp. 12–13.

Father of all,
we give you thanks and praise,
that when we were still far off
you met us in your Son and brought us home.
Dying and living, he declared your love,
gave us grace, and opened the gate of glory.
May we who share Christ's body live his risen life;
we who drink his cup bring life to others;
we whom the Spirit lights give light to the world.
Keep us firm in the hope you have set before us,
so we and all your children shall be free,
and the whole earth live to praise your name;
through Christ our Lord.
Amen.[31]

The opening section refers to a homecoming, where the Son is sent to meet us; Christ has done this through his death and resurrection in which we participate through the Eucharist. It is possible to understand this prayer at the surface level of the text in the way just outlined; however, the worshipper may be alerted to the presence of an intertext by the ambiguity of the opening statement. Does the sending of the Son refer to the incarnation? From where were we far off? What home were we brought to? The competent reader, that is the worshipper familiar with scripture, will recognize here an allusion to the parable of the Prodigal Son which concludes with the unworthy, penitent and hungry son returning to his father's house and expecting to work as a slave, but instead is greeted by his father and the homecoming celebrated with a banquet (Luke 15.11–32). Now, the worshipper who is able to identify this intertext will notice the verbal parallels 'still far off . . . brought us home', but she will also notice that the intertext is not faithful to the parable – in the prayer it is Christ who has been sent to meet us, in the parable it is the father. The intertext works to produce meaning despite the 'mistake' because, in the appropriation of the parable and in the prayer, the worshipper is able to identify herself with the prodigal son. Thus the scripturally competent worshipper in praying this prayer will be affected by the parable's message of God's loving

---

[31]CW, p. 265.

kindness in forgiving sin and will respond appropriately with the gratitude suggested by the prayer, that, like the prodigal, she 'was dead and has come to life; he was lost and has been found' (v.32). A worshipper who is able to identify the presence of an intertext and then access it is able to situate themselves in another narrative, which will inform their self-perception at the moment of utterance.

A collage from scripture

Although there are probably other types of liturgical intertexts to be identified and explored apart from this final type which shall be discussed here, they are likely to be variations on quotation, paraphrase and allusion. There is though the phenomenon of a collection of scriptural verses being read or sung without alteration or comment. In the visual arts items of different colours and textures may be combined to form a single image, which we call a collage; so too in literary texts, a combination of quotations taken from different and unrelated sources may form a verbal collage in which meaning is derived from the whole rather than the parts. An example familiar to Anglicans would be the opening of the Burial Service in the Book of Common Prayer, where a selection of biblical quotations accompany the entrance of the body into church:

I am the resurrection and the life, saith the Lord: he that
believeth in me, though he were dead, yet shall he live:
and whosoever liveth and believeth in me shall never die.
St. John 11.25, 26.

I know that my Redeemer liveth, and that he shall stand
at the latter day upon the earth. And though after my
skin worms destroy this body; yet in my flesh shall I see
God: whom I shall see for myself, and mine eyes shall behold,
and not another. Job 19.25, 26, 27.

We brought nothing into this world, and it is certain
we can carry nothing out. The Lord gave, and the
Lord hath taken away; blessed be the name of the Lord.
1 Tim. 6.7; Job 1.21

These are clearly identified as intertextual elements by the biblical references given in the Prayer Book but, unlike scriptural readings (lections), they are overtly liturgical elements, demonstrated by the rubric that they accompany a liturgical action. They are not offered for study or for exposition, nor even really for meditation. In the service they function to recollect the congregation before God for the task to come. Indeed it is the effect of their recitation, and the familiarity of the words which adds structure and security to the worshippers' experience. It is clear from their lack of narrative that they are from different parts of the Bible, but it is not necessary for the worshipper to know the source texts in order to get what they are saying. The texts have been chosen to express the church's belief in the resurrection of all believers and present a theology of death. They have been placed in a specific order, which does not follow their place in scripture. It is the cumulative effect of these sentences which carry the meaning, and not their individual parts; the parallel with a visual collage becomes obvious.

Conclusion

As one reflects upon intertextuality in the context of the liturgy, it is possible to recognize more and more texts which contain elements borrowed from other texts. These may be explicitly indicated by textual or verbal signs, or be hidden in a liturgical text as an allusion. These elements are incorporated as part of a deliberate authorial strategy to express and create meaning, but once in the world the author is no longer able to control what meaning the worshipper may make from them. There are so many variables at play in the interpretative process: the worshipper may or may not identify an intertext; she may choose not to ignore it and concentrate only on the surface of the text; she may identify an intertext but have no idea of the source text; she may identify the intertext with another text known to her but not intended by the author. We have noted, though, that the dominant source text in liturgical texts is the Bible and so within the shared cultural context of the Church, both authors and worshippers have a better chance that their meanings will converge; although even then the scriptural source text may be mediated through hymns and other liturgical texts.

One of the challenges which has faced liturgical authors and translators in recent decades has been the decline of biblical literacy among the general population and even within many congregations. Thus intertextual elements which may have worked in the past may not do so any longer. Additionally, lectionary revisions have resulted in large parts of the Old Testament never being heard and New Testament and gospel readings have been reduced to mere snippets, all of which lessens the opportunities for worshippers to hear the source texts upon which the liturgical texts rely for their meaning. Thus attention to intertextuality provides us with a further example of how meaning may be generated or missed in the worship event and how authorial intention and worshippers' interpretation may not always converge.

6

Language

Some of the most contentious debates in many churches over the last decades have been over the language used in public worship: over the translation from Latin and seventeenth-century English to contemporary English; over gendered and hierarchical language; over perceived (in)comprehensibility. Current debates, as I write, over the retranslation of the *Roman Missal* into English indicate that not much has been resolved and that, if anything, the battle lines are more clearly drawn. This chapter will not repeat aspects of those debates which are, in any case, easy to locate and too voluminous to summarize, but instead will look more closely at how language functions in the liturgical event and how the distinctive context of worship causes the adoption of specific linguistic features. Lastly, though, we will consider the notion of 'style' in relation to liturgical texts.

The function of language in liturgical worship

Language, expressed in written texts which are then spoken, constitutes the principal part of a liturgical event. Of course rituals, music, place and people also constitute the event and are communicative acts; however, it is the words which are the constant and shared feature of the liturgy. What is it, then, that language distinctively does in worship? What is its function?

Communication of meaning

Language functions as a means of communication in worship, just as much as it does in other areas of life. Worshippers communicate with each other, individually and collectively, they communicate to God, and there is a presumption that God also communicates with them. Formal features such as dialogues between the minister and people, the 'Word of the Lord' proclaimed in the readings, intentional one-way communication in the sermon or the intercessions, etc., make this abundantly clear. Communication is, though, about meaning and not simply words. In scripture and in the tradition there are frequent warnings about 'vain repetition', that worship is not the utterance of formulae, but the expression of intentional meanings from the heart, which may be in words but can also be in deeds. Attention to the communication of meaning, and not words, moves us away from the surface of the text to note that language is a conduit for meaning and not an end in itself. As we shall see below, there are some words which are used in a technical sense and here the specialist interpretation is required; however, communication of meaning is at the level of the sentence and not individual words, it is also conveyed by the context and by ritual. Thus the statement, 'We break this bread to share in the body of Christ'[1] requires the worshipper first to accept that 'bread' is being used technically in this context to mean 'the large wafer in the priest's hands', secondly that only one member of the congregation is 'breaking' the bread, and thirdly that the 'sharing in the body of Christ' only happens in this particular context and not at the parish lunch afterwards. The meaning is then not the sum of the meanings of each individual word, but of the whole utterance within a specific context.

Edification

The Preface to the 1662 Book of Common Prayer emphasizes that one function of the liturgy particularly dependent upon language is the edification of the people:

> whereas Saint Paul would have have such language spoken to the people in the Church as they might understand, and have profit

---

[1]CW, p. 179.

by hearing of the same; The Service in this Church of *England* these many years hath been read in Latin to the people, which they understand not; so that they have heard with their ears only, and that their heart, spirit and mind, have not been edified thereby.

And, again,

> Though it be appointed, That all things shall be read and sung in the Church in the *English* Tongue, to the end that the Congregation may be thereby edified; yet it is not meant, but that when men say Morning and Evening Prayer privately, they may say the same in any language that they themselves do understand.[2]

Here, the liturgical language must be comprehensible to those participating so that its meaning is clear. The BCP is silent whether any aspects are more edificatory than others and about the fruits of edification. Attention to this aspect of worship, though, does not imply a simplistic liturgical language, but it does require that the meaning is potentially accessible and that obfuscation and obscurantism ought to be avoided.

There is a confusion in much of the liturgical language debate about the relationship between the complexity or comprehensibility of language and the complexity of meaning thereby conveyed, which, given the impossibility of expressing the mystery of God is a task inevitably doomed to failure. However, choosing language which is not immediately accessible means that worshippers, of whatever level of education and linguistic skill, will be required to unpack the sentence before unpacking the meaning: that is, they have to translate the liturgical text into something they can understand and the liturgy may as well be in a foreign language. This is also a theological issue. Christ conveyed complex ideas, the meaning of which appears to be difficult to unravel as the mountain of books produced by New Testament scholars attests, but did so using the images and language of everyday – someone keeping pigs, looking for something valuable that has been lost, lighting a lamp and then

---

[2]Book of Common Prayer (1662): 'Concerning the Service of the Church'. <http://www.churchofengland.org/prayer-worship/worship/book-of-common-prayer/con-cerning-the-service-of-the-church.aspx> [accessed 29 July 2013].

blocking out its light, and, of course, leaving to the church as a memorial of his Passion the ordinary stuff of bread and wine. Thus it should be of no surprise to theologians that the everyday can convey the things of the greatest significance and complexity.

Articulating experience of God

Liturgical language is not just about God, but it is addressed to God and brings those who use it into the presence of God such that God may speak through the liturgy. The language we use in public prayer, enables us to a variable extent, to articulate our experience of God; it provides us with vocabulary for 'God-talk'. It may also provide us with a language for our own prayers, the manner of addressing God, or of making petitions; it presents to us attitudes to God and about the world which we may model in prayer and in our lives, attitudes of gratitude, praise, love, repentance, for example. It is not surprising then that those charged with the provision of liturgical texts receive such diverse and strongly felt responses to their work, precisely because the liturgical texts facilitate the personal as well as the communal relationship with God.

Makes present that of which it speaks

Liturgical texts are composed on the basis of theological presuppositions about God, about humanity, about the ordering of creation, about the relationship between people, and between people and God. Exclamations like 'Lord have mercy' are not just requests made in hope and are not commands, but are pre-fulfilled requests made in the knowledge of a merciful God derived from promises in the gospels and validated by the experience of worshippers or the community. Through language, distinctions between God and humanity are established. Traditionally, this was by reserving 'Thee/Thou/Thine' for God after it had fallen out of use between people in spoken and written English, but even now certain epithets are reserved for God which are not used of humans or even heavenly beings – 'ineffable', for example. When used in the liturgy, an epithet like 'ineffable' does not describe God or conjure up God by clever wordplay, rather it asserts that the God who is present in the liturgy is recognized as ineffable, or immortal, or almighty. These words restate for the community what sort of God it is who hears and answer their prayers.

In the 1970s there was considerable interest among sacramental theologians in the 'Speech-Act Theory' of J. L. Austin who proposed that speech was not just used to convey information but that speech could constitute an action in itself.[3] The liturgical example Austin used was 'I declare you man and wife': this statement does not describe an existing situation, but brings the situation into existence. Thus Austin distinguished between 'constative' language, that used to convey information, from 'performative' language. In the latter, statements have 'illocutionary force', that is what the statement effects is independent of its semantic content. For Jean Ladrière and others this theory offered considerable insight into the operation of liturgical language.[4]

The illocutionary force of liturgical language is complex: it is exhortative, confessional, interrogatory, it includes statements of belief, wishes, and imperatives.[5] Ladrière explored the threefold performativity of language in relation to the liturgy as 'existential induction', as 'an institution' and thirdly as 'presentification'. 'Existential induction' concerns the way in which the external form of the language awakens in the worshipper certain affective dispositions: Ladrière refers to the way in which the typical personal pronouns used in liturgy, us and thou/you, indicate the places occupied by the speakers in relation to what is spoken. Verbs too, those of asking, praying, giving thanks, etc., and some imperatives imply a non-expressed performativity. For example, 'Lord hear us', really means 'Lord we beg you to hear us'. These illocutionary acts presuppose certain attitudes between the speaker(s) and the addressee – trust, veneration, gratitude – which come into effect at the very moment when they are spoken. The use of 'performative' is significant, the liturgical words do not describe an action or an attitude, but constitute the action itself.

---

[3] J. L. Austin, *How to Do Things with Words* (2nd ed. Oxford: Oxford University Press, 1975).
[4] Jean Ladrière, 'The Performativity of Liturgical Language', *Concilium* 9, no. 2 (1973), pp. 50–62.
[5] Ibid., p. 54.

Secondly, Ladrière noted that the effect of liturgical language as 'an institution' disposes souls to welcome that which it suggests and thereby institutes a community. When 'we' is used in a liturgical text it brings into existence a community which did not exist before it was uttered. He writes, 'Language is not the expression of a community constituted before it and apart from it and is not the description of what such a community would be, but the location in which and instrument by means of which the community is constituted.'[6]

The most fundamental aspect, according to Ladrière, is that of 'presentification': it is an act of the language to make present for the participants that of which it speaks – that is the mystery of Christ, of his life, death and resurrection. The language does not merely describe or picture these things, but endows it with particular operativity by means of (a) repetition, (b) proclamation and (c) sacramentality. The liturgy repeats texts which announce the mystery of salvation as that which has or is to come; it is not merely quoting but resuming into the present words which were written/ spoken in the past. Proclamation is demonstrated most powerfully in the creed and confessions of faith where the illocutionary force is that of attestation, ratification or commitment.[7] In sacramentality, liturgical language has its most profound actualizing effect. When the words of Christ at the Last Supper are repeated it is more than commemoration; these words receive again the very efficacy which they had when Christ himself used them, they confer the power to do what they mean, but the realization of what is spoken is effected by faith and not by the language.

Jean Ladrière provides a very useful analysis of the specific way in which language works in the liturgy in relation to faith and the sacramental presence of Christ in the worshipping community. The words do not describe, they manifest, and thus for him they are endowed with a sacramentality because some of these words spoken now in the liturgy have the same efficacy as when they were spoken by Christ. Thus in the liturgy, through language, the Church makes assertions about a reality perceived by the participants, it wishes for that which it believes is achievable (healing, the kingdom of God, etc.). Within the conditions created by the liturgy these things are true and real, and the liturgy creates the context where these

[6]Ibid., p. 59.
[7]Ibid., p. 61.

can credibly be requested. To pray 'Thy Kingdom come' presumes a pre-existing notion of what the 'Kingdom' is, to acknowledge its desirability and to place oneself within it; this Kingdom exists already, but paradoxically will also come. To speak about it in the liturgy is, then, to make it a present reality and does not simply describe a state of affairs.[8] In worship, participants, both speakers and hearers, assent to the reality of what is said potentially or actually, whether or not they experience the fulfilment of what is prayed for or about.

Identity formation

The Church is established by its liturgy, primarily through the sacraments of baptism and Eucharist and through the normative status of scripture. In worship the Church realizes herself, and Christians are formed. As words dominate worship, they do therefore become the means through which the community understands itself, worshippers create bonds between them and individuals find articulation of their place in the body of Christ. In certain secularized Western cultures, a worshipper's identity may be acutely formed and distinguished by the use of an exclusive language. The social linguist Andrée Tabouret-Keller has remarked that 'Members of a group who feel their cultural and political identity threatened are likely to make particularly assertive claims about the social importance of maintaining or resurrecting their language.'[9] The role of language in identity formation and preservation may well be the principal driver of the somewhat interperate language debates in the some churches. To maintain a preference for Church Slavonic, or Latin, or sixteenth-century English as the language for public prayer may well be about a reaction to contemporary society and/or its threats to the church, rather than theological or aesthetic arguments. However, even worship in a contemporary idiom uses language in distinctive ways which mark out the activities of the worshipping community from those outside the worship context.

---

[8]Ibid., p. 60.
[9]Andrée Tabouret-Keller, 'Language and Identity', in Florian Coulmas (ed.), *The Handbook of Sociolinguistics* (Oxford: Blackwell Publishing, c. 1997), p. 318.

The liturgical context and language

The vernacular is the language that I use, for me that is English; however, I use it in different ways depending upon which context I am in. I possess a range of vocabulary and employ it in different contexts to create utterances with different meanings, but also with different styles. All users of their native language will speak differently to their children than to their children's teachers. We recognize that vocabulary and style change as context changes but nevertheless we would assert that we are speaking the same language. We use written language in a manner quite different from our spoken language: we write lists, notes or prose using a whole range of devices which are hidden in speech, such as punctuation or paragraphing. Our schooling has made much of this automatic and unreflected. To say that the liturgy is or ought to be in the vernacular is therefore to say something more than about what language should be used, one must consider as well what vocabulary and style will be most appropriate in the context of the worship.

Collective speech

The distinctive feature of liturgical language from any other type of speech event in our culture is that it is collective speech; it is not the speech of an individual nor of a collection of individuals, but it is the speech of a group. This has two stylistic effects: that in syntax, rhythm and vocabulary it may be easily spoken; and that the meaning conveyed has the potential to be assented to by all. It is normal in all churches, whether using a set liturgical text or not, for people to participate in liturgical events using words which they have neither chosen nor composed; in order to do so, they have suspended the very subjectivity which they may employ in everyday life in other cultural and social activities. The liturgy is shared prayer, shared speech, never the possession of an individual or a group composed of individuals asserting their individuality. But the responsibility for ensuring that this shared collective prayer may take place is not just on the participants, but also on the liturgical composers and leaders. Liturgical texts might prefer language which can be easily spoken in a physical sense by participants, but they need to employ language which can be spoken, that is carry the assent, however tacit, of the participants.

Speakability

Liturgical language is spoken, but the composers of texts have not used the sort of language we might use in conversations between friends, or even in more formal situations, such as a public speech. Although texts are written for speech, they are not intended to replicate ordinary speech in the way that the script of a television soap opera may; a closer parallel might be theatre, a much more stylized speech, but even that is neither like ordinary language, nor exactly like written language.

Contemporary worship, on theological grounds, has placed an emphasis on the 'fully conscious, and active participation' in the liturgy by the people[10] and consequently comprehensibility and speakability have become key concerns in the provision of all liturgical texts, but particularly those for the congregation to speak. Congregational texts are usually intended for choral recitation which, in order to avoid cacophony and barriers to participation, require attention to rhythm, 'speakability' and opportunities to breathe, even before one attends to the accessibility of the meaning.[11] 'Speakability', here, describes what remains when any barriers to physical speech are removed, that is avoiding words of five or more syllables, avoiding awkward sequences of consonants or sibilants, avoiding tongue-twisters.

Choral recitation also works much better when sentences are broken up into short phrases with a regular rhythm which also helps them be easily memorized. The printed text may indicate when the congregation can breathe by presenting the text in broken lines with disregard to normal written language conventions, particularly the integrity of the sentence and punctuation. In particular, liturgical texts may employ a rather idiosyncratic system of punctuation, with an excessive and non-standard use of commas, semicolons

[10]*Sacrosanctum Concilium* 14. <http://www.vatican.va/archive/hist_councils/ii_vati-can_council/documents/vat-ii_const_19631204_sacrosanctum-concilium_En.html> [accessed 30 April 2013].
[11]David Crystal and Derek Davy, *Investigating English Style* (London: Longman, 1969), p. 149.

and colons. Thus, for example, in the BCP, the Lord's Prayer is
punctuated in a manner which makes the sentence construction
unclear:

> Our Father, which art in heaven, Hallowed be thy Name. Thy
> kingdom come. Thy will be done in earth, As it is in heaven.
> Give us this day our daily bread. And forgive us our trespasses,
> As we forgive them that trespass against us. And lead us not into
> temptation, But deliver us from evil. Amen.

And then again in longer congregational texts, the *Gloria*, creed and
Te Deum for example, lines may be broken or unexpected colons
inserted. Thus the *Te Deum* in the BCP opens like this with colons
used to indicate a pause and not a new semantic unit:

> We praise thee, O God : we acknowledge thee to be the Lord.
> All the earth doth worship thee : the Father everlasting.

And in *Common Worship*, the creed begins like this with line breaks
to help recitation but which disrupt the flow of the prose:

> We believe in one God,
> the Father, the Almighty,
> maker of heaven and earth,
> of all that is,
> seen and unseen.[12]

   Despite this sort of injury to sentence construction for the benefit
of speech, liturgical texts do not reflect normal speech patterns: they
avoid contractions such as 'isn't' and 'won't', inarticulate interjections
like 'um' and 'er', and the sort of incomplete utterances that we find
in conversations. When worship leaders depart from the 'script', such
as in extempore prayer, intercessions or when giving notices about
community events, then some semblance of normal speech patterns
may return, although even here conventions about the type of language
proper to each communication activity may displace normal speech.
There is what may be called a 'formality' to what people are expected
to say, even when using the contemporary idiom.

---

[12]CW, p. 173.

Distinctive too is the manner of speaking: choral recitation requires a much flatter intonation than one might use when reading aloud or speaking in other contexts. This flat intonation is also present when the minister speaks alone or an individual reads extracts from scripture, even when there is animated dialogue or strong emotion. The speakers opt for clarity over meaning, corporate seemliness over personal expression: think what it might sound like if the congregation did, in fact, 'bewail our manifold sins and wickedness' as the general confession from the Book of Common Prayer suggests they ought![13] So, another feature of liturgical language is that the performance of the text may not be connected to its content or intended meaning.

In most acts of worship, the words which are spoken or sung have not been written by the speakers, and unlike a play intended to be performed by professional actors, the speakers in worship are likely to be an extremely diverse group in terms of age, race, culture, education and regional accent. This poses particular problems for those charged with providing those words who may choose a style of language close to contemporary speech patterns even though exhibiting some formality, or indeed acknowledging that the language of the liturgy will always display features which are alien to a particular group at any one time, may self-consciously adopt a style which is quite different than normal. Perhaps the recognition that liturgical language continually departs from everyday language and the attendant risks of losing comprehensibility is indicated by the work of historical as well as contemporary liturgical reform movements. Thus the Preface to the 1662 BCP justifies the changes from the earlier books because of the need

for the more proper expressing of some words and phrases of ancient usage in terms more suitable to the language of the present times, and the clearer explanation of some other words and phrases, that were either of doubtful signification, or otherwise liable to misconstruction.[14]

---

[13]BCP, 1662. <http://www.churchofengland.org/prayer-worship/worship/book-of-common-prayer/the-lord%27s-supper-or-holy-communion.aspx> [accessed 21 August 2013].

[14]Preface to the BCP, 1662. <http://www.churchofengland.org/prayer-worship/worship/book-of-common-prayer/the-preface.aspx> [accessed 21 August 2013].

The diversity of communication activities

Not only are the speakers themselves diverse, but liturgical worship also employs a very broad range of communication activities and, in addition to those features already mentioned, the form and style of language changes with each activity. First, ministers or leaders speak alone to God on behalf of the congregation or on their own behalf, or they address the congregation directly, there may be dialogues with the congregation; the congregation as a whole or through a single representative may address the minister, or each other or God. The purpose of the communication also varies considerably: to praise God, to make requests, to express sorrow or joy, to convey instructions, to tell stories, to state beliefs. Even when the content may change from week to week, texts often follow established patterns (genres) which affect the way the information is presented and the choice of vocabulary; this is most clearly demonstrated by collects or Eucharistic prayers or certain forms of intercession. Spoken texts can follow prose patterns, but texts intended for singing are often in metre where the music's demand for rhythm and rhyme may further override normal syntactical conventions. In addition to music, the words may be accompanied by rituals which extend the meaning beyond what the words at face-value indicate; an obvious example of this would be the Eucharistic prayer. Or at baptism, where the meaning of 'I baptize you in the name of the Father, and of the Son and of the Holy Spirit' can only be completed by a ritual action involving water. Such diversity might not even be found in the entire output of a speech radio station, but in churches it is contained within a single worship event.

Technical vocabulary

In common with all other groups in society, the church employs 'technical language' either by using certain words or phrases which are not used anywhere else, or by giving a distinctive meaning to ordinary words. Examples of such technical vocabulary include theological terms like consubstantial, redemption, bless, but also ordinary words such as bread, cup, peace, man. Additionally, there are partially anglicized loan words from languages unfamiliar to the congregation like baptize, Eucharist or presbyter, and it is not

unusual for many diverse congregations to be comfortable with the
Greek prayer *Kyrie eleison, Christe eleison, Kyrie eleison.*
Other 'exclusive' language exists because of the heavy borrowing
of imagery and metaphors from biblical texts. As we have discussed
in Chapter 5, these might be present in direct quotations, such
as 'Holy, holy, holy Lord', in a modified form like the institution
narrative in the Eucharistic prayer which conflates the accounts
in the gospels and I Corinthians 11, or just as allusions. Although
the predominance of agricultural imagery may seem archaic in
(post-) industrial societies, their presence is legitimate because
drawn from the community's primary narrative, the Bible, which
it owns and celebrates every time it worships. Attempts to provide
contemporary imagery, for example Richard G. Jones's 1968 hymn
'God of concrete, God of steel'[15] have had a highly polarizing effect,
or the US Episcopal Church's 1979 Eucharistic Prayer C, dubbed the
'Star Wars prayer' because of the thanksgiving for 'the vast expanse
of interstellar space, galaxies, suns, the planets in their courses, and
this fragile earth, our island home':[16] these are considered unusual.
Liturgical texts employ, then, vocabulary and imagery which is
not common in the surrounding culture but which is used without
comment by worshippers because it is part of their culture infused
by scripture and their own traditions. But is this an indicator of a
distinctive language, or simply a style of language belonging to a
subculture?

In addition to vocabulary and imagery, worshippers employ
forms of greetings which are unusual outside the worship context.
Many liturgies begin by the minister addressing the congregation
with 'The Lord be with you' to which the response is 'and also
with you' or 'and with your spirit', rather than 'Good Morning' or
'Hello'. In English Anglican practice, this brings about the curious
feature of the vicar 'greeting' the congregation at the church door
after the service with 'hello' and a handshake, where 'The Lord
be with you' would be considered extremely inappropriate. And
whereas it would not be considered appropriate to say 'hello' to

[15]Richard G. Jones, 'God of Concrete, God of Steel', *Hymns Ancient and Modern,
New Standard* (Norwich: Canterbury Press, 1983), no. 366.
[16]The Episcopal Church, *The Book of Common Prayer* (New York: Church
Publishing Inc., 1979), p. 370. <http://www.episcopalchurch.org/sites/default/files/
downloads/book_of_common_prayer.pdf> [accessed 21 August 2013].

someone several times during a conversation, this liturgical address may be used three times in one service without attracting comment. Similarly, the liturgy may close with 'Go in peace', rather than 'Bye, then' or 'See you next week'.

Again unlike normal speech situations, the one addressed is almost always named in the liturgy, often with additional epithets. The most common form of the addressee is 'God', 'Father', 'Lord', to which can be added 'almighty', 'merciful', 'loving', 'eternal'. The epithets may be doubled to produce, for example, 'Almighty and everlasting God', and then subordinate clauses may further elaborate the characteristics of the addressee, for example 'Eternal God, giver of love and power . . .'.[17] Only in liturgical texts is the distinctive form of address 'O . . .' retained, even in contemporary liturgical books. It is not just God, but worshippers too who are directly addressed and named in unique ways. The Book of Common Prayer, for example, contains some quite distinctive forms of address for the people, the most well-known would be from the opening to the Marriage Service: 'Dearly beloved, we are gathered together . . .'. Modern English texts, though, have tended to remove such terms when these introductory paragraphs are revised and worshippers are now usually addressed impersonally. Thus the same text in the 1980 *ASB* opens with 'We have come together . . .';[18] similarly in *Common Worship*, which, by and large, removed the prefaces. Such a change is more than simply about modernizing the language, afterall one might easily expect partners to address each other with something like 'John, dear, pass me the newspaper'. Social and ecclesial changes are indicated where those present at a Marriage Service may well not be members of this or any worshipping community and thus an ambiguity is introduced about their place in it – can they truly be 'dearly beloved'?

A further distinction between the forms of address in the liturgy and outside is the absence of 'politeness formulae' such as 'would you be so kind as to . . .', or the ubiquitous 'please and thank you' of much British English; mostly absent too are deferential terms, 'Sir' or 'Madam', used between the participants (a rare example might be the scripted exchanges between a deacon and a bishop in the Orthodox liturgy), and formulaic terms of endearment which

---

[17]Post-communion prayer for the Sunday after Ascension, *CW*, p. 477.
[18]*ASB*, p. 288.

are used regardless of kinship – 'Dearly beloved in Christ . . .', 'My brothers and sisters . . .' and not 'Ladies and gentlemen' for example.

Normative meanings

In the last chapter we noted the extent to which liturgical texts were dependent upon quotations and allusions to scripture and that this text forms the bedrock of normative religious language about God for the Christian community. As Crystal and Davey have noted liturgical texts cannot depart from normative doctrinal formulations without the risk of charges of heresy and this places a further restriction upon language choice.[19] An interesting linguistic consequence of the need for orthodoxy is the way in which statements are qualified by additional information in subordinate and relative clauses, by additional adjectives. So for example, in the BCP collect for Ash Wednesday:

> Almighty and everlasting God, *who hatest nothing that thou hast made and dost forgive the sins of all them that are penitent*; Create and make in us new and contrite hearts . . .

David Hillborn noticed that this was even a feature of extempore prayer in the historic free churches where it serves to 'load further the dogmatic ballast', sometimes so extensively that the purpose of the prayer may be completely obscured![20]

Self-referential

Webb Keane noted the way that ritual speech constantly reminds the participants and restates what the action is and what it means.[21] This might be illustrated by the words at the fraction: 'We break this bread to share in the body of Christ/Though we are many we

---

[19]Crystal and Davey, *Investigating English Style*, p. 149.
[20]David Hillborn, *'The Words of our Lips': Language Use in Free Church Worship* (London: Congregational Memorial Hall Trust, 1998), pp. 25–6.
[21]Webb Keane, 'Religious Language', *Annual Review of Anthropology* 26 (1997), p. 50.

are one body because we all share in the one bread.'[22] He calls this 'metapragmatic' and suggests that 'One reason is presumably that the supposed participants do not all share the same spatiotemporal context, or do not share it in quite the same way.'[23] That is, unseen divine and heavenly beings are believed to be present, and are invoked to participate and act in the rituals. This raises the paradox that in order for these metapragmatic statements to make sense, there is an expectation that the participants have some prior knowledge and experience which they draw upon, but if that is indeed the case then the repetition of such statements, when accompanied by the relevant ritual action, is somewhat redundant.

Style

'Style' is a contested concept because it carries with it an implication about normative language, or elevated prose or speech used among an educated elite. One could use 'register' instead or a descriptive term like 'variety' or 'type' and then avoid the inherent subjectivity of the term 'style'. But, I have deliberated chosen to use 'style' because of the way in which the extremely intemperate and, by now, highly politicized debates about what sort of language should be used in worship are conducted, during which opinion, prejudice and personal preference have replaced any genuine seeking for common ground. Given that, 'style' seems an eminently appropriate term to employ.

Gail Ramshaw has noted how many congregations appear to cope only too well with a mixture of language styles:

> Sometimes in a single Sunday liturgy, but surely in the assemblies of a single community, we hear a cacophony of voices: the seventeenth century Lord's Prayer, 'Creator, Redeemer, Sustainer', Thee's and you's, praise songs in which Jesus is my friend, traditional translations of 'Adoro Te Devote' and back to Latin via Taizé.[24]

---

[22]CW, p. 179.
[23]Keane, 'Religious Language', p. 50.
[24]Gail Ramshaw, 'The Pit, or the Gates of Zion? A Report on Contemporary Western Liturgical Language', *Worship* 75, no. 1 (2001), p. 13.

As Ramshaw summarizes, and experience tells us, worshippers are happy to use languages and language styles in the liturgy which are quite different from their everyday language. Where decisions have been made to replace traditional with contemporary language, the choice of which style of contemporary language should be used has provoked much disagreement. Underlying these disputes is the fundamental question of whether there is such a thing as 'liturgical language'. Do the linguistic features discussed in the previous section constitute a distinctive form of the language, or is it that the liturgical context determines linguistic choices which are only unique in so much as they are combined in that context? Should we speak about 'liturgical language', or 'language used liturgically'? And, if the former, might we wish to further distinguish it from the everyday by calling it a 'sacred language',[25] or a 'ritual language'?

The problems facing revisers and translators when choosing a style are pretty much the same, although choices are often more implicit when already working in the target language, whereas translators are required to choose a specific variety of the target language, as well as determine the extent to which the original should make its presence felt in the translated text. Lynne Long has remarked on the problems of translating 'holy texts' in that 'the space it needs in the target language is often already occupied'.[26] For English, this space is occupied by the Book of Common Prayer which is used as a model for other denominations as well as Anglicans. In a comparison of

---

[25] *Liturgiam authenticam*, issued by the Roman Catholic Church in 2001, required that vernacular liturgical texts should be 'free of an overly servile adherence to prevailing modes of expression' and that following the guidelines in this document might lead to the development of 'a sacred style that will come to be recognized as proper to liturgical language. Thus it may happen that a certain manner of speech which has come to be considered somewhat obsolete in daily usage may continue to be maintained in the liturgical context' (LA 27). <http://www.vatican.va/roman_curia/congregations/ccdds/documents/rc_con_ccdds_doc_20010507_liturgiam-authenticam_En.html> [accessed 29 July 2013]. This should be contrasted with the previous guidance for translations in *Comme Le Prévoit* (1969) which stated that, 'The language chosen should be that in "common" usage, that is, suited to the greater number of the faithful who speak it in everyday use, even "children and persons of small education",' and the vocabulary was to be 'normally be intelligible to all, even to the less educated' (CP 15). <http://www.ewtn.com/library/CURIA/CONSLEPR. HTM> [accessed 29 July 2013].

[26] Lynne Long, 'Introduction' to ibid. (ed.), *Translation and Religion. Holy Untranslatable?* (Clevedon: Multilingual Matters Ltd, 2005), p. 1.

modern translations of the *Liturgy of St John Chrysostom* for the
Greek Orthodox Church in Britain, Şerban noted that the BCP
was a preferred model for one produced as recently as 1982 for a
monastic community. Obviously there was no culturally determined
variety of English proper for Orthodox worship and thus translators
were required to make a choice; in this case they chose an archaized
English. Şerban accounted for this by the text's primary use within
a fixed community of liturgy professionals (monks) and noted that
it would have been unsuitable for the alternative context of mixed
congregations of non-native speakers of English, second-generation
immigrants and British converts and so a translation produced for
use in the parishes did not employ any archaisms.[27] Eamon Duffy
too held up the BCP as a model for the revised translation of the
Roman Catholic Sacramentary. In an article which was critical of the
prosaic and simplistic English of the 1973 *Missal*, he demonstrated
that the Latin text could have been translated in the manner which
Cranmer employed, for nearly identical texts in some cases, and
that it was possible to do so without archaizing. The features of
Cranmer's liturgical style held up for imitation included repetitions
and synonyms, and Duffy was critical of the 1973 translation of the
Missal for its use of short and simple sentences which flattened out
complex ideas and broke up the rhetorical structure.[28]

Those who write decrying contemporary language liturgies often
complain about the lack of some aesthetic qualities – the language is not
beautiful, it is prosaic, turgid, etc. They compare it with the culturally
normative liturgical language of the the BCP or the Latin mass, or
Church Slavonic, and conclude negatively that it cannot convey the
transcendence of God. Strategies may be employed to enable the
retention of historic forms – a contemporary text may be provided
in archaic as well as modern language (see *Common Worship*, Holy
Communion Order Two), or an apologetics is proposed based upon
explaining words which no longer exist or whose meaning has shifted,
or even having to explain the whole liturgical text. Adriana Şerban
cites Susan Bassnett who explains the reason for choosing archaic

---

[27]Adriana Şerban, 'Archaising versus Modernising in English Translations of the
Orthodox Liturgy: St John Crysostomos in the 20th Century', in Long, *Translation
and Religion*, p. 77.
[28]Eamon Duffy, 'Rewriting the Liturgy: The Theological Implications of Translation',
New Blackfriars 78 (1997), pp. 15–20.

language is to convey 'remoteness of time and place'[29] and Nida, who said that it served to 'strengthen historic associations, but also heighten the mystery of religious expression'.[30] Şerban commented that such a choice is bound by a belief in the appropriateness of 'distancing' the worshipper from God, which she concludes 'is linked to a particular ideology about the religious genre, rather than being an objective observation'.[31] In the polarized debate, stances are taken in relation to a perceived either/or choice between transcendence and immanence. G. L. Bray even made the theologically rather astonishing criticism of those who think that 'God should be found in the marketplace – not just present there, in some hidden way but found there, in the normal course of life.'[32]

Conclusion

Hopefully the earlier parts of this chapter have demonstrated that there are distinctive features about the liturgical context which have an effect on the type of language used, these relate to the formal, visible linguistic features found at the surface level of the text and to the function of language in the liturgical event. Aesthetical considerations may well come into play once these more fundamental aspects have been adhered to, but to start with the aesthetic can only serve to place the textuality of the liturgy above the liturgy as event and encounter. This is not to dismiss such considerations as they may be useful to aid the daily and weekly repetition of texts, the memorizing of them by worshippers which ultimately cause them to form a foundation for corporate and personal spirituality. By necessity, texts which are owned by a group are less fluid than our own speech, less prone to change, and thus the language of liturgical worship will always and necessarily be out of step with contemporary speech patterns and idiomatic use. This may not be problematic, so long as criteria such as edification, comprehensibility and participation are not compromised.

---

[29]Susan Bassnett, *Translation Studies* (London and New York: Routledge, 1991), p. 72, in Şerban, 'Archaising', p. 82.
[30]Eugene A. Nida, *Towards a Science of Translating* (Leiden: Brill, 1964), p. 179, in Şerban, 'Archaising', p. 84.
[31]Şerban, 'Archaising', p. 84.
[32]Gerald L. Bray, *Language and Liturgy*, Latimer Studies 16 (Oxford: Latimer House, 1984), p. 11.

7

Paratext

As we have remarked earlier, it was a radical step of Thomas Cranmer to provide a single book for all liturgical events in the Church of England and simultaneously abolish the plethora of medieval service books. Anglicans have been particularly attached to this book as an object; it was widely owned, given at Confirmation and carried to church even if it remained unopened. As a child I spent many sermons investigating the list of people I would not be able to marry and trying to decipher the tables for finding the date of Easter, although I had very little idea how to follow the liturgy using the very same book. The liturgical book contains so much more than the liturgical text (which here we will define in a restrictive sense as that intended be spoken in worship).

When considering the liturgical text as the result of the intentional creation of an object, we need also to consider the way in which it is presented and how that presentation may affect its use in the worship event. It is these objects which are thrust into the hands of a worshipper at the church door and in order to use them effectively the worshipper requires not just sufficient literacy but also technical skills in understanding how the book, or other printed material, functions in relation to their participation in the liturgical performance. Not all churches rely on the literacy and technological skill of their congregations, out of tradition or innovation. Of the former, in Orthodox churches it would be extremely rare for any laity but the choir to have a text in front of them; however, the clergy require numerous different books which are often taken from shelves in the sanctuary and thus not available to the laity at all. In Roman Catholic churches it would still be uncommon, although increasingly not unusual, for the laity to come with a missal; the congregation's relatively fixed role at Mass means that the congregational texts are often recited from memory. In churches where worship leaders have the freedom to devise and lead the worship as they see fit there may be no shared liturgical material at all, although the increasing use of electronic resources may mean the worshippers have access to snippets of liturgical text but will not necessarily know what will follow or how they are connected using textual strategies alone. Given the variety of worship events at which a liturgical text could be required, for illustration we shall confine ourselves to the main Sunday Eucharistic service in churches with set forms of liturgy, but our observations would apply equally to other contexts where a printed liturgical text was provided for all.

The thresholds of the text

We are warned not to judge a book by its cover, but that is exactly what we do. Not just its cover, but its name, author, size and presentation. When we begin to read we are influenced by the aids to that reading – typeface, page layout, divisions, ease of locating the required sections. None of these features constitute the text itself, they are introductory, or explanatory or simply follow the conventions for presenting printed material. Gérard Genette has described all these features as the 'thresholds of the text'. They are the means by which we access or enter the text, but do not constitute the text itself; Genette calls them 'paratexts'.[1] In what follows we will draw upon Genette's discussion of the various paratextual elements with the hope that by concentrating on the way in which we receive the text of our liturgies, we will make explicit the textual strategies and technologies which worshippers require.

When we are confronted with a liturgical book, we first encounter the cover. Passing through that we may then find these conventional features: the half title page; the title page; legal, ecclesial and publication data; a list of contents; a preface or introduction. None of this belongs to the liturgical text or is required for worship; it is what makes the text a book. As Genette remarks, 'it extends the

---

[1] Genette, *Paratexts*. Originally published in French in 1987 as *Seuils*.

text in order to present it'.[2] Similarly, if we turn to the back of the book, we shall encounter the cover and inside blank pages; an index; a list of references; additional publication information, etc.; these conclude the liturgical text, but do not constitute it. Between this opening and concluding material is, we hope, the liturgical text itself – but where? The book may well contain the texts for more than one liturgical event, which requires separation by headings, and these events themselves may be further divided by levels of subheadings to indicate their constituent parts. Surrounding, or sometimes within, the liturgical text will be rubrics differentiated by typeface and/or colour. Each page may well have numbers and other information at the top or bottom. The book is likely to provide a separate section containing instructions and information about the conduct or interpretation of the liturgy; there may be a lectionary or calendar presented as a table; and sometimes an illustration. None of this does or ought to form the text used in the liturgical event but it cannot be denied that all these paratextual elements have varying degrees of influence on the performance, interpretation and, when the congregation has the book open in their hands, upon participation.

Genette noted that the paratext shares the characteristics of the text, that is 'it is itself a text; if it is still not *the* text, it is already some text'.[3] The reader is required to pass through, or over, the paratext in order to access the text, but of course if one were to remove these distinguishing visual aids, then the reader would be entirely reliant upon other textual clues, such as 'Chapter 1', to indicate where the text commences. The conventions for publishing novels make it relatively simple to identify the threshold, but liturgical books display a much more complex paratextual apparatus and so if we ask our question 'where does the liturgical text start?' of the Church of England's core liturgical book we might well have to search a bit harder.

Common Worship: Services and Prayers of the Church of England begins with eleven pages of various information numbered in roman numerals (explicitly vii to xi) and a blank red page, before arabic numerals begin with page 1, which is a conventional indicator that the opening remarks have ended. What commences

---

[2]Ibid., p. 1.
[3]Ibid., p. 7.

on page 1, though, is 'The Calendar', indicated by the title at the top of the page, but followed only a direction to further rules on page 526 and an instruction for interpreting the typeface used in the calendar itself. Is this where our liturgical text commences? Nothing in the following pages 1 to 17 would be spoken in a liturgical event, although admittedly it would directly affect the content of worship. Page 18 is again a blank red page, and page 19 carries the hopeful heading 'A Service of the Word, Morning and Evening Prayer, Night Prayer'; however, page 19 only contains a list of contents for this section. Page 20 is a blank white page. Page 21 begins three pages of an introduction to 'The Service of the Word', which as it 'consists almost entirely of notes and directions and allows for considerable local variation and choice within a common structure'[4] is entirely without any liturgical text at all. The following pages (pp. 24–27) contain structural outlines and notes. Page 28 is another blank red page. Page 29 is titled 'Morning and Evening Prayer on Sunday' and contains a theological and liturgical introduction, and, at last, on page 30 we find the first liturgical words:

Grace, mercy and peace
from God our Father
and the Lord Jesus Christ
be with you.[5]

Now, after forty pages, we have arrived at what is unequivocally 'liturgical text'. This example is not untypical.

Much of this preliminary material is what Genette placed in the category of 'peritext', a spatial and material zone which 'exists merely by the fact that the book is published'.[6] So too that which is found at the end of the book. This might contain publisher's information, an index, the back cover with its barcode and ISBN number. Genette noted that the peritextual feature of the book cover is directed at the general public, but as one moves further into

---

[4]CW, p. 21. All the paratextual features of *Common Worship* can be viewed in the electronic versions of the printed texts (in PDF format) on the Church of England website <http://www.churchofengland.org/prayer-worship/worship/texts/common-worship-pdf-files.aspx> [accessed 26 August 2013].
[5]CW, p. 30.
[6]Genette, *Paratexts*, p. 16.

the book and, say, arrives at the preface one is almost a reader of the text; by contrast that which occurs at the end of the text (save the back cover), is directed at someone who is already a reader. This concluding material is also at the threshold of the text: it starts where the text has just concluded. Liturgical books also contain this concluding peritextual material and, starting with the outside back cover we can move inwards to the threshold of the text again.

It is unusual for a liturgical book to have any text on the back cover, this is most likely in imitation of leather-bound books which restricted cover material to the spine alone; the inside back cover and slip are also invariably left blank. The Book of Common Prayer, in some editions, may have printing information on an otherwise blank page, if there are blank pages before the cover; but it is more usual for the inside back cover to be blank and the preceding page to contain 'A Table of Kindred and Affinity wherein whosoever are related are forbidden by the Church of England to Marry Together'. Helpfully, at the end of this table in the edition before me as I write are the words 'THE END' (original italics and capitals). These then are the concluding words of the book, but they do not follow anything which might be heard in a liturgical event. Between the last liturgical words in the Accession Service and 'The End' are to be found the 'Royal Warrant for the Accession Service' and the 'Thirty-Nine Articles': twenty-five pages of material in all. Common Worship: Services and Prayers has thirty-five pages of concluding material after the final liturgical texts of the canticles. Here we find a page of 'Authorization Details' (pp. 815–22), 'Copyright Information' (pp. 817); 'Acknowledgements and Sources' (pp. 818–22); an 'Index of Biblical References' (pp. 823–36); and a 'General Index' (pp. 837–50). Although they are expanded here, some aspects of the authorization and copyright details have already been dealt with on pages iv and vii; the acknowledgements function rather like endnotes; the biblical and thematic index imitate that found in most theological publications and are a curious inclusion in a liturgical book. Most of this concluding material one might expect to find in an academic text book, which raises interesting questions about the sort of generic models favoured by the publishers and authors.

When we pose the question, 'where does the liturgical text begin and where does it end?', we will receive a confused answer if we assume that the book and the text are coterminous. We can see that liturgical books follow normal publishing conventions with regard

to the peritext;[7] *Common Worship: Services and Prayers* displays
contemporary publishing styles, except for the almost empty covers.
Genette was primarily concerned with novels which, even though
the peritext might be extended by multiple prefaces or introductions,
do at least normally start on page 1. We can see that liturgical texts
are buried among considerable introductory and supplementary
material, not just in the book, but also in the provision for each
liturgical event, where an extremely complex paratextual system
operates. So in addition to the peritext for the book, each liturgical
event requires its own peritext which will comprise a range of
the following: title page; notes; rules; instructions; structure;
contents; a 'pastoral introduction';[8] a 'theological introduction';[9] an
'introductory note',[10] etc. They may also have their own concluding
peritext: 'supplementary texts'; 'seasonal provisions'; 'notes'; an
'annex',[11] appendices; 'a selection of additional prayers',[12] etc. All of
these, apart from 'notes', do contain texts to be used in the liturgical
event, but are not presented in a manner which facilitates that,
functioning rather as a compendium of variable liturgical units.

Having, I hope, drawn your attention to the extent of the
paratextual material surrounding liturgical texts, which has been
placed there by the intentional actions of the publisher and author,
we turn to consider how they function as a communication between
author and reader, even though they hopefully do not form any part
of the communication between worshippers.

Authors and readers

Genette asks us to consider the 'situation of communication' which
at the very least operates at the level of the title of the book,[13] but

---

[7]Genette (*Paratexts*, p. 13) noted the power of convention. A similar list is found in
Common Worship: Pastoral Services, although curiously there is no index of biblical
references.
[8]*CWPS*, pp. 102 and 256.
[9]Ibid., p. 9.
[10]Ibid., p. 12.
[11]*CW*, p. 245.
[12]*ASB*, p. 334.
[13]Genette, *Paratexts*, p. 73.

then operates more generally every time a paratextual element directs the reader towards a particular use of a liturgical text. In Chapter 2 we discussed what 'authorship' might mean in relation to liturgical texts, and in liturgical books we note that paratextual declarations of authority and authorization demonstrate once more the diffused way in which authorship is attributed. All *Common Worship* volumes carry a prominent page (a right page with prominent 'level 1' title) called 'Authorization' which lists the authorities for the contents of each book (the Book of Common Prayer, General Synod, or the House of Bishops) and reminds the (unidentified) reader of the restrictions placed upon the local church under Canon B3.[14] The *ASB*, however, did not use roman numerals and the pagination surely began with the half-title page, although the first number is on the page containing publication information presented as '4/*History*' (original italics). Here there is no attempt to separate text from paratext by numerical means. The 'Authorization' appears in very small typeface, on a left-page, at page 8; what might be the 'situation of communication' here? We could surmise that in 1980 the 'sender' (the Bishops, General Synod or the Liturgical Commission) assumed that the unnamed recipient would not need to be reminded of Canon B3; whereas in 2000 the sender quite obviously knew that the implied readers would need to be so reminded. This would seem to be confirmed by the additional presence in *Common Worship: Services and Prayers* of the legal formula of the 'Declaration of Assent' made by all in recognized ministries at ordination or licensing; the Declaration concludes, 'and in public prayer and administration of the sacraments, I will use only the forms of service which are authorized or allowed by Canon'.[15] The situation of communication indicates, somewhat strangely, that the authors are not at all confident that the implied readers will use the book and its texts!

Who are these implied readers? In the copy of the Book of Common Prayer in front of me, probably printed in the 1990s, there is a hint that this book is intended for a layperson. On the three pages preceding the title page are 'How to follow the Service. Morning Prayer', 'How to follow the Service. Evening Prayer', 'How to follow the Service. Holy Communion' with, on each page, a

---

[14]See for example, *CW*, p. vii.
[15]*CW*, p. xi.

structural outline of each service with page numbers. One notes that the owner of the book is encouraged to 'follow' the service and not participate in it. Such concern with, albeit limited, lay participation is unusual as not even in contemporary Church of England books, where 'fully conscious, and active participation' might reasonably be presumed, are there any guidelines directed specifically at them.[16] That the laity are not the intended readers may be further illustrated by rubrics attached to liturgical texts where, typically, the words to be spoken by the congregation are indicated by '*All*' (italics and red type) in the left margin, whereas words which the minister must (or should) say are without any such indication. Optional words to be spoken by the minister are preceded by the rubric '*The minister may say*' (italics and red type) but now with the same indentation as the liturgical words.

Titles

What is the purpose of a title? All liturgical books have titles: some are simply descriptive and are related to the function of the book or its contents; others situate the book in relation to other books; some, and this is the case with more creative liturgical works which are not 'official', bear no relation to either content or function. We do need to assume that the title is chosen with care and intention; that is, the author expects it to mean something to whoever they think the recipient/reader might be. But, as Genette remarks, although the author may have a particular reader in mind, the title is available to anyone whether they read the book or not.[17] The title is also a distinguishing feature, separating this book from all other books, but as Genette comments this can be done just as easily by an ISBN code![18] Of course a title may be chosen to entice or attract a purchaser, but it has to be said that that does not seem to have

---

[16]These words were used in *Sacrosanctum Concilium* 14 issued by the Second Vatican Council in 1963, although they have been adopted as liturgical principles by all the historic Western churches. <http://www.vatican.va/archive/hist_councils/ii_vati-can_council/documents/vat-ii_const_19631204_sacrosanctum-concilium_En.html> [accessed 26 March 2012].
[17]Genette, *Paratexts*, p. 75.
[18]Ibid., p. 80.

been a consideration of those publishing official liturgical books, in distinction to those popular collections of prayers published without official approval.[19]

The title of a liturgical book is often likely to contain some sort of genre indication; that is the word 'liturgy' or 'worship' or 'prayer' or 'services' and this is the case for official and unofficial publications. But there are other distinctive features in titles. One notes that some churches feel obliged to include the name of their church or denomination in the book title, thus: *Methodist Worship Book* (1999); *Lutheran Book of Worship* (1994); *The Book of Common Order of the Church of Scotland* (2005). Some churches do not need to: Roman Catholic books are known simply by their liturgical function *Roman Missal, Pontifical, The Divine Office*. Some liturgical books have a dual title, the main title which is that by which the book will become known and a subtitle which is more specific. Thus, if we compare the three principal books of the Church of England we will note that 'Church of England' is contained in a subtitle and not the main title, and does not form part of the name by which it is popularly known (Table 7.1).

In the two twentieth-century books there is a deliberate and conscious reminder of the authority of the Prayer Book, a feature of titles which Genette called 'connotative', that is they 'provide the text with the indirect support of another text, plus the prestige of cultural filiation'.[20] So, the *Alternative Service Book* reminds readers that the BCP is still authorized and has not been supplanted, and the subtitle reinforces this, and 'Common' is retained in *Common Worship* even though 'common' denotes different things in the two books. In the BCP, the extremely long and descriptive subtitle indicates that the referent of 'common' is not the whole collection of liturgical material provided in the book; 'common prayer' is distinguished from 'sacraments' (baptism and holy communion),

[19]A brief search on the website of an internet book merchant indicated that although 'A collection of prayers' often forms the subtitle, the titles of popular prayer books can vary considerably and none of them have an obvious connection to the function of the volume; for example, Marsha Maurer, *In the Garden. A Collection of Prayers for Everyday* (Uhrichsville: Barbour Publishing, 2000); Kathryn Hayes, *From my Heart to His. A Collection of Prayers* (New York: iUniverse, 2004); Arthur Bennett, *The Valley of Vision. A Collection of Puritan Prayers and Devotions* (Edinburgh and Pennsylvania: Banner of Truth Trust, 2002).
[20]Genette, *Paratexts*, p. 91.

TABLE 7.1 *The titles and subtitles of Church of England liturgical books*

Popular name	Title	Subtitle
BCP, The Prayer Book	The Book of Common Prayer	And administration of the sacraments and other rites and ceremonies of the church according to the Church of England together with The Psalter or Psalms of David pointed as they are to be sung or said in churches; and the manner of making, ordaining and consecrating of Bishops, Priests and Deacons
ASB	The Alternative Service Book 1980	Services authorized for use in the Church of England in conjunction with The Book of Common Prayer together with The Liturgical Psalter
Common Worship	Common Worship	Services and Prayers for the Church of England

'other rites and ceremonies' (presumably churching, commination, marriage and funerals), 'the psalter' and the ordination services. By a process of elimination, therefore, '*Common* Prayer' can only refer to Morning and Evening Prayer and the Litany; it did not refer to the whole range of authorized liturgical events of the Church of England, as is the intention in *Common Worship*. A further connotive feature in the *ASB* is the date, an echo of one popular name for the BCP, 'the 1662'. A missing connotive element from *Common Worship* is, ironically, the word 'book'!

Titles are also used to indicate affinity between books in a series, and we would presume this to be the intention behind the fairly uniform use of *Common Worship*. Each volume in the series is prefixed with '*Common Worship*' followed by a colon and then '*Pastoral Services*', '*Christian Initiation*' or '*Daily Prayer*'. The unity of the series is maintained by typographical design, but not by the design of the cover; they are each a different colour and some have different dimensions. Additionally, the title on the spine is inconsistently horizontal or vertical. *Common Worship: Services and Prayers* has only 'Common Worship' placed horizontally, whereas the others continue with the subtitle placed vertically – might this be intended to indicate some sort of relationship between them? Apart from the title there would be little to indicate to the uninformed that they were a series. We might further remark that 'Common Worship' does refer to the book or books and not to the activity presumed to follow from using the book, as *Common Worship: Ordination Services* would seem to indicate.[21]

Intertitles

If the book title is directed at the general public, the internal titles are directed at the reader; for these Genette coined the neologism, 'intertitles'.[22] They serve to divide the text into blocks by theme, arranged according to some sort of sequential logic and are one of the means by which an author guides the reader through the text. An intertitle can be placed at the head of a part, section, chapter, part of a chapter and even a paragraph and there is no convention about the amount of text which might be placed beneath it. Genette did note, however, the tendency for texts intended for, or derived from, oral delivery to be without intertitles: 'the very fact of oral performance would make it hard to indicate the presence of intertitles'.[23] Modern liturgical texts, however, are awash with intertitles, but it would be a most incompetent minister who read them aloud, so what is their function in relation to the liturgical text and for whom are they intended?

Each liturgical event has its own name and that invariably occurs at the head of the collection of relevant liturgical material and in the 'Table of Contents'. Such titles are descriptive of the act of worship to which they relate: 'Morning Prayer', 'Holy Baptism' and in the three

---

[21]In the BCP, the ordinal was not part of the common prayers and, being an episcopal liturgy, it is to be found in the *Roman Pontifical*. My point here is that an examination of the paratextual elements of CW indicates a diminution of the role of the laity. How 'common' is an exclusively episcopal and clerical act?

[22]Genette, *Paratexts*, p. 294.

[23]Ibid., p. 295.

Anglican books they have remained fairly static over the centuries. Some titles of course are theologically and ecclesiologically loaded and none more than those provided for the Eucharist (Table 7.2).

A section intertitle can also be used for 'running heads', that is at the top of the each of its pages, or 'feet' at the bottom, and the choice of which of the multiple names for the Eucharist is chosen should be seen as indicative of the author's preference. In the BCP, the running head is reduced to 'The Communion'. In both the *ASB*

TABLE 7.2 *Titles for the Eucharist in Church of England liturgical books*

Book	Title in list of contents	Title at head of the liturgical material
BCP, 1549	The Supper of the Lord and Holy Communion, Commonly called the Mass.	The Supper of the Lord and Holy Communion, Commonly called the Mass.
BCP, 1662	The Order for the Ministration of the holy Communion	The order of the administration of the lord's supper or HOLY COMMUNION
ASB	The Order for Holy Communion Rite A (or Rite B)	The Order for Holy Communion also called The Eucharist and The Lord's Supper Rite A[a]
CW	Holy Communion	*The Order for the Celebration of* Holy Communion *also called* The Eucharist *and* The Lord's Supper[b]

[a]*ASB*, p. 113.
[b]*CW*, p. 155.

and *CW* there are running 'feet': '*page number/Holy Communion A*'
consistently in the *ASB*;[24] but in *CW*, the left hand page reads '*Holy
Communion*' (italics and red) but the right contains an abbreviated
version of the subsection title, thus '*Order One: Eucharistic Prayer
A*', or '*Supplementary Texts: Penitential Material*'.[25] We shall return
to the relationship between these variable footers and their section
titles below.

Earlier we sought to find the liturgical text in the liturgical book,
now we search for it on the page by distinguishing the liturgical text
from paratext. As in this book I have divided chapters into sections
by inserting intertitles, so too on the pages of many liturgical
books do we find intertitles to highlight particular liturgical texts
or to divide a particular liturgy into distinct elements. The use of
these is not neutral and by typeface, size and position the author
communicates the hierarchical ordering of text which lies beneath
it. In the entire BCP Communion service there are only two such in
headings: 'The Collect' and 'Proper Prefaces'. They are indicated by
capital letters, centred on a separate line than the rest of the text,
but the function of each intertitle is quite different. 'The Collect'
occurs before the invariable and opening 'Collect for Purity' not
the variable collect for the day, whereas 'Proper Prefaces' occurs
before the five variable prefaces. The use of such titles in the BCP
is relatively modest and the liturgical text is mainly interrupted by
rubrics.

In complete contrast *Common Worship* is awash with intertitles
of various types (see Figure 7.1). Those responsible have said that
the reason for the two principal headings was twofold: 'The ranged-
right heading style means that someone following the service
through from beginning to end is not disturbed by frequent intrusive
headings. By contrast, someone leafing through to find a particular
element can do so quickly by scanning down the right-hand side
of the page; here the headings are prominent.'[26] The intertitles and
their hierarchy in *Common Worship* are more complex than those
responsible may have imagined and here I shall try to establish

[24]*ASB*, p. 115ff.
[25]*CW*, p. 184ff. and p. 275ff.
[26]Colin Podmore, 'The Design of *Common Worship*', in Bradshaw (ed.), *Companion*,
vol. 1, p. 257.

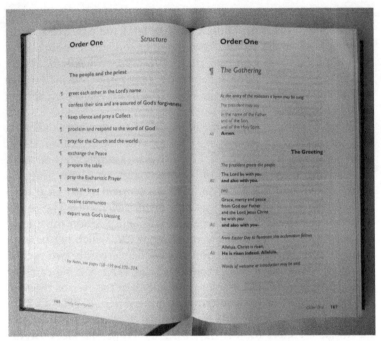

FIGURE 7.1 *Paratextual features of Common Worship: Services and Prayers (pp. 166–7), reproduced with permission.*

what they are before drawing some conclusions about the 'situation of communication' they imply.

The highest level of intertitle is that which functions like a chapter heading and these we shall call 'level 1' titles. What is found under these titles is material for a particular liturgical event, or a collection of liturgical material, or information, and they are preceded by a blank red page which further emphasizes that the reader has moved to a new section. Thus we find them at the beginning of material for a single liturgical event – 'The Order for the Celebration of Holy Communion, also called The Eucharist and the Lord's Supper'; or for a series of related liturgical events – 'Service of the Word, Morning and Evening Prayer, Night Prayer', or supplementary material – 'Collects and Post Communions', or even rubrics – 'Rules'.[27] Except in the case of the Eucharistic material, the

---

[27]CW, pp. 19, 155, 375, 525.

volume's contents page lists these intertitles using exactly the same words. Intentionally or unintentionally, the author has emphasized the Eucharist by presenting the title in both red and black typeface on its own on page 155 (other level 1 titles are followed by rubrics or a list of contents on the same page), and by leaving the overleaf blank. Thus the titles indicate a hierarchy which is not evident from the order in which the sections occur: the Eucharistic material is placed about a quarter of the way into the book.

Because beneath most of the level 1 titles lies a collection of liturgical material, these are further distinguished by a lower level of title which is also placed in a contents list for that section and used as a running foot.[28] These 'level 2' intertitles refer to material for a liturgical event – 'A Service of the Word', 'Morning and Evening Prayer on a Sunday', as well as for liturgical texts – 'The Litany', 'Authorized Forms of Confession and Absolution'.[29] They are printed in black bold type and left justified, whether they are on the left or right page; on the contents page they are also in black bold type.[30]

Beneath the level 2 titles are further divisions of the material provided, either by genre or by its sequence in the liturgical event. These do not appear in the contents list for the whole volume, although they are in the separate contents list for 'A Service of the Word' etc. and 'Holy Communion';[31] they are also distinguished by not being in bold type although there is considerable inconsistency about their inclusion in running feet.[32] On the page they are in red, not bold but in italics, left justified and preceded by a pilcrow (¶). As with the others, these 'level 3' intertitles may also refer to liturgical material such as 'Forms of Intercession', or for rubrics, 'General Notes', and are used for

---

[28]The word 'Contents' in each section is right-justified and in red, see *CW*, p. 157. The running feet are consistent on left and right pages except in the Eucharistic material.

[29]Ibid., pp. 21, 29, 111, 122.

[30]Ibid., p. 19.

[31]Ibid., pp. 19, 157.

[32]As is becoming apparent the use of titles is somewhat inconsistent, as are the running feet: in the Eucharistic material the level 3 titles appear as 'sub-titles' in the feet on both pages; under the level 2 title 'Authorized Forms of Confession and Absolution', the level 3 title 'Confessions' appears as a foot on left pages only, and 'Holy Baptism' is an invariable foot.

the outline 'Structure' of a liturgical event.[33] In the baptismal and Eucharistic material, level 3 headings refer explicitly to the principal structural elements of the liturgy – 'The Gathering', 'The Liturgy of Baptism'.[34]

Unfortunately, there is yet a further level beneath the level 3: titles which denote liturgical texts themselves or the structural elements of the liturgical event. 'Level 4' titles, such as 'Readings', 'Sermon', 'The Blessing',[35] are in bold, black typeface but right-justified. They are listed in the 'Structure' of each liturgical event.

The levels we have identified with their typographical hierarchy, do not relate to the hierarchy which will be imposed upon their contents in the liturgical event. Some level 1 titles refer to single liturgical events, others to a number of events related in some way, others to collections of liturgical material. Level 2 titles, again, are used for specific liturgical events or for collected material; and level 3 is again used for an event, or collected material or for instructions. Only under level 4 titles do we finally come close to liturgical texts and units presented in a similar way as they would be used in worship. In general though, this paratextual system bears no relation to an act of worship. Worshippers without the *Common Worship: Services and Prayers* would be unaware of all this – and they would be most fortunate; however, those with the book before them are likely to find their use directed by the author's hierarchy of material rather than the actual act of worship. None of the intertitles indicate what the author considers to be the climactic moment of any of the liturgical events for which the book is intended. Arguably, the climactic moment in the Eucharist is the act of Communion which in Order One is subsumed below '¶ *The Liturgy of the Sacrament*' (level 3), below 'Giving of Communion' (level 4), after a series of prayers, in a rubric saying 'The priest and people receive communion'.[36]

Page and section numbers

In addition to intertitles, liturgical books may employ numerical systems of ordering the material they contain. It is common

---

[33]CW, pp. 158, 281, 348.
[34]Ibid., pp. 167, 352.
[35]Ibid., p. 363.
[36]Ibid., p. 181.

to find page numbers, but some additionally assign paragraph numbers to prayers and rubrics separately. The purpose of this is to facilitate the location of relevant sections in the preparation of worship but they also risk intruding into the liturgical event and in some cases even become liturgical text. Page and paragraph numbers are a purely visual and printed phenomenon so it is curious that worship leaders have relied upon them to direct worshippers to the relevant texts rather than using the name of the text or unit. It was not uncommon for the Church of England Eucharistic liturgy from the *ASB* to commence with an announcement that 'The service begins on page 119', and one might still hear 'We say together the prayer our Lord taught us on page x, Our Father . . .'. Such intrusions of the paratext into the liturgical text and the liturgical event only serve to further highlight the perception that the liturgical text, that which is spoken, and the liturgical book are coterminous.

Notes and rubrics

In *Common Worship* liturgical text is buried under four levels of titles (more could easily be identified but establishing distinguishing criteria is not so straightforward), but also under rubrics and other advisory material. The titles and intertitles contain implicit messages from the author to the readers, but more explicit messages are conveyed in the more formal sections titled 'notes', 'rules', 'instructions' and in the dispersed rubrics between liturgical texts. These are found much closer to the liturgical text and directly affect its use; they also influence or control the liturgical event and its interpretation. Notes and rubrics imply liturgical and theological perspectives, they may be those of the denomination or of the individual or group responsible, but in no sense can they be considered neutral. The supreme example in Anglican liturgical history is the last minute insertion of the 'Black Rubric' into the 1552 BCP which contains ritual and theological instruction in justification of kneeling to receive communion and rejects that 'any adoracion is doone, or oughte to bee doone, eyther unto the Sacramentall bread or wyne there bodily receyved, or unto anye reall and essencial presence there beeyng of Christ's naturall fleshe and bloude.'[37] Not all rubrics are as explicit as this, but nevertheless they indicate the theological, liturgical and ecclesiological preferences of the author.

Rubrics can be differentiated according to the type of information they convey. Three principal types can be identified: those which concern the speaker of the liturgical text; those which concern liturgical action; and those which influence the choice of liturgical texts. Additionally, we need to distinguish between rubrics and 'notes' or 'instructions'. In modern liturgical books, a rubric accompanies the liturgical text to which it applies and is situated at the point where it is to be followed, whereas 'notes' or 'instructions' are gathered together at the beginning or end of the material for a liturgical event and give guidance on the whole or significant parts of the liturgical event. The former affect the liturgical event at the time of its performance, the latter affect the preparation of that event but would not be consulted during it.[38]

The most frequently occurring rubric indicates who is to speak the text to which it is attached. In *Common Worship: Services and Prayers* we can remark that the congregational texts are preceded by 'All' placed in the margin; however, 'President' or 'Minister' is never a marginal rubric but is most frequently contained in a sentence like, 'The President says . . .' above the text which is to be spoken. Presidential texts are commonly distinguished by the further typographical feature of not being in bold, whereas congregational texts are in bold. Who may speak in a liturgical event is theologically loaded; churches which have a sacramental priesthood insist that certain words and actions are reserved to ministers of an appropriate rank. The rubrics reflect this position. Thus, in *Common Worship* a variety of ministries are mentioned: 'President', 'priest', 'minister', 'the reader' (one who reads, not a Reader); these are distinguished from 'the people', 'candidates' (at baptism) and 'all'. It is most notable that in a church which continues with the threefold ministry that in this book there is no rubric for the deacon: the gospel is read

---

[37]BCP (1552), Holy Communion <http://justus.anglican.org/resources/bcp/1552/Communion_1552.htm> [accessed 27 March 2012].

[38]In CW, rubrics are in red and attached to the text to which they refer, usually under a level 4 heading; notes and instructions are in black under level 3 headings separate from the liturgical texts.

by a 'reader' and the dismissal by 'a minister'.[39] 'Minister' is used in a very imprecise manner: in non-sacramental liturgies and in the plural it always implies any authorized minister, lay or ordained; however, its use in Holy Communion serves to distinguish parts which the President may delegate. The *Roman Missal* distinguishes much more clearly between the words to be spoken by the priest and those of the people to the end that the role of the people in the liturgy is much more clearly defined. Who speaks the text is almost always contained within a sentence or clause, thus: 'The people acclaim' or 'The people reply'. And this is more marked when the rubric concerns the priest or other minister whose instruction to speak is accompanied by a ritual instruction; for example, 'The Priest, turned towards the people, extending and then joining his hands, adds: . . .'.[40] In the *Missal* ritual speech and ritual action go together; in *Common Worship* the absence of ritual instructions risks further isolating the liturgical text from the liturgical event. One notes too that the *Missal* has a greater variety of named ministries: *sacerdos*, *diaconos*, *epsicopos*, *minister/minsitris*, *cantatur*, *lector*; the congregation are referred to most often as *'populus'* but sometimes also as *'fideles'*.[41] The use of the very unspecific 'All' in *Common Worship: Services and Prayers* risks weakening the autonomous activity of the laity and the congregation in the liturgical event. We can see this in dialogues where the proposer is also a responder:

The president . . . says
The peace of the Lord be always with you
All: and also with you.[42]

And of even more concern at the conclusion of the Eucharistic prayer where the 'Amen' is a congregational response to the prayer spoken on their behalf by the priest; again, preceding 'Amen' with the rubric 'All' disenfranchises the congregation.

[39]See *CW*, pp. 172 and 183. Unsurprisingly, the distinctive ministry of the deacon does appears in *Common Worship: Ordination Services* (2007).
[40]*Order of Mass*, §127, from *The Roman Missal, English translation according to the Third Typical Edition* (Dublin: Veritas, 2011).
[41]See *Missale Romanum ex decreto sacrosancti oecumenici concilii Vaticani II instauratum auctoritate Pauli PP. VI promulgatum Ioannis Pauli PP. II cura recognitum, Editio typica tertia* (Vatican City: Typis Polyglottis Vaticanis, 2008).
[42]*CW*, p. 175.

The second category of rubric is that which directs the ritual actions of the ministers, individuals or the congregation and these ritual actions may additionally involve the use of liturgical items or of specific locations. Traditionally, Anglicans have been sparing in such rubrics, whereas the Roman Catholic liturgical books are more explicit. An examination of the Roman Catholic 'Rite of Baptism for Children' reveals rubrics which instruct the priest to face the people he is talking to (candidates, godparents, congregation); those which refer to the movement of people in the liturgical space (processions into the church, to the font, to the altar); those which refer to actions involving liturgical items (oil, water, candle, baptismal robe). Again, the presence or absence of a ritual action is theologically motivated as one can see in early Anglican debates about the retention of the sign of the cross or the use of oil in baptism.

Lastly, rubrics control the choice of text to be spoken by stating whether and what sort of permitted variations there are, and by directing the reader to required variations such as seasonal material. Of surprise to members of other reformation churches, it is notable that the BCP contains not one rubric about hymns and consequently it was a long time before Anglicans felt comfortable using them. Some rubrics are permissive whereas others are not. Thus under the level-4 intertitle 'Preparation of the Table. Taking of the Bread and Wine' in *Common Worship: Services and Prayers* are five rubrics of which three are permissive and two are obligatory, for example:

A hymn may be sung.

The president takes the bread and wine.[43]

Throughout the text 'may' is used to indicate a permissive rubric, but the indicative active tense for obligatory rituals.

Conclusion

Liturgical books have become complex texts which require the reader, in addition to basic literacy, to appropriate specific 'reading technologies' in order to release text for use in the liturgical event.

---

[43]Ibid., p. 175.

In common with other books they must negotiate front and end matter, the organizing strategies of titles and numbers and then, unlike novels or cookery books, be directed in the way in which they are to read the text once they have found it. The brief examination of *Common Worship* indicates that this is a book which contains quite a number of the features which would be found in the genre of a textbook or reference book, and as we noted above in relation to the titles, its use in an actual worship event was only one of the considerations affecting the organization of material. In the worship event, it is to be hoped that the 'situation of communication' is between the worshippers and God, but paratextual elements establish another 'situation of communication' between the author and the worshippers. Although not present in the event, the author's voice may well be the only one to be clearly heard.

8

Worship

In the previous chapters we have investigated the text from behind and before so to speak, the explicit and implicit processes by which it has been produced and how these affect the interpretation of the text in worship. During a liturgical event participants may be reluctant to admit that their worship is directed by this text, presuming that somehow worship is a state of being, whereas the text by which it is facilitated is merely a material object. However, their attention may be drawn again and again away from worship as an ontological state to more earthly concerns about what is to be said and done by explicitly textual and literary elements such as scripted dialogues, announcements like 'The reading is taken from . . .', or even by the minister providing page references. These text-referential elements both constitute the ritual situation and also stand outside it to draw attention to themselves by alerting the worshippers that full participation requires textual competency. As Webb Keane remarked, these self-referential elements do make it obvious that something different is going on even if they offer no interpretation and are not meaning-laden.[1]

Unlike other sorts of texts, such as a theological treatise, a sermon, some sorts of stories, neither the liturgical text nor its performance presents information logically which proceeds from A to B in an ordered way. Wade Wheelock referred to the 'choppiness of liturgical texts', and that liturgies 'lack . . . cohesiveness' because

---

[1]Webb Keane, 'Language and Religion', in Alessandro Duranti (ed.), *A Companion to Linguistic Anthropology* (Oxford: Blackwell Reference Online, 2005). <http://www.blackwellreference.com/subscriber/tocnode.html?id=g9781405144308_chunk_g978140514430822> [accessed 31 July 2013].

they are designed for a ritual context.[2] To make sense of the liturgy, then, worshippers necessarily require some prior experience so that they can accept the non-standard speech patterns, the non-sequential transfer of information, the culturally incongruous allusions, in order to potentially find new meanings in 'a fixed text (meaning a written document, memorized set of utterances, or traditionally prescribed pattern) that is known or accessible to the participants before they engage in the performance of the rite'.[3] Experienced participants will not consciously reflect on this, but they will at least be aware that their ability to follow what is going on improves with familiarity; similarly, when confronted with the liturgical text, they are unlikely to consciously reflect on the required literacy skills. Facilitating meaning-making, but also to an extent masking the required competencies, is the ritual context where physical movement and gesture, the space, music, etc., combine with the text to produce the realities of which the text speaks, as Wheelock noted 'each utterance is seen as presenting or bringing into being some element of the predetermined situation that the ritual re-enacts'.[4] The combination produces an ever repeatable 'situation', and thus because the primary function of language here is not to convey information, he suggests that cognitive engagement is not of primary importance, but rather participation.[5] Following this final comment from Wheelock, we have identified three issues in need of further reflection to attempt to clarify the role of the text in worship. These are the repetitive aspect of the liturgy and how that alerts us to the textuality; the nature of participation when a text guides the worship; and the way in which the text generates meaning.

Textuality and repetition

Unlike the transcript of a parliamentary debate, a liturgical text has only a tenuous link to an original speech event, and unlike the

---

[2]Wade T. Wheelock, 'The Problem of Ritual Language: From Information to Situation', *JAAR* 50, no. 1 (1982), p. 50.
[3]Ibid., p. 58.
[4]Ibid., p. 62.
[5]Ibid., p. 63.

script of a soap opera, it is not intended to be an imitation of a
real speech event; however, both of these share with the liturgical
text the potential to reconstruct the words of the event long after
it has happened. What we hope distinguishes the liturgical text is
that, in the context of worship, the repetition of the words brings
about a completely new event, the text therefore always has a future
orientation and potentiality: it is not complete by being inscribed
or printed on a page and is only fulfilled in future indeterminable
performances. How can we make sense of this aspect of repeatability
in relation to the authenticity of the worship event?

The 'Speech Act' theory, proposed by J. L. Austin and refined
by John Searle and others,[6] usefully showed how language is not
just used to convey information but that it does something, that
is certain types of statements effect that which they contain. Key
examples cited by Austin were statements such as 'I promise' or 'I
bet', and he also included the quasi-liturgical example 'I declare you
man and wife'.[7] These statements he defined as 'performative'. The
issue then arises: what is the performative aspect (i.e. what happens)
when performative statements are used in the theatre or at wedding
rehearsals? We would naturally say that the actors are not married
during the play and the couple are not married at the rehearsal, but
that a marriage comes about only during the real thing. Austin called
these other uses of the performative 'parasitic' and 'infelicitous', and
described them negatively in relation to the 'original' and effective
use.[8] Jacques Derrida, however, took particular exception to this
negativity in relation to 'infelicitous' repetition; for him such use
was integral to the statement and not a misuse of it.[9] Only if it had
validity in one context could it be redeployed in another, and this
is especially the case with written texts which have repetition, or
'*iterabilité*', built into them. This discussion is relevant to liturgical
texts given that it is not uncommon for some Christians to consider
repetition in worship as 'vain' (Matthew 6.7) and, we shall see, it
will also help us reflect further on the role of the text in worship.

---

[6]Austin, *How to Do Things*; John R. Searle, *Speech Acts: An Essay in the Philosophy of Language* (Cambridge: Cambridge University Press, 1969).
[7]Austin, *How to Do Things*, pp. 5–6.
[8]Ibid., p. 22.
[9]Jacques Derrida, 'Signature Event Context', in idem., *Limited Inc* (Evanston: Northwestern University Press, 1988), pp. 13–19.

Derrida pointed out that, because of the very fact of its being written, recorded and not simply spoken in the present moment, a written text has a life independent from either its writer or its intended recipient. When we write something down we intend to make permanent that which is only fleeting in a conversation, we record it so it can be retrieved later in circumstances where the author and the intended recipient are absent. Thus, he says, 'In order for my "written communication" to retain its function as writing, i.e. its readability, it must remain readable despite the absolute disappearance of any receiver, determined in general. My communication must be repeatable – iterable – in the absolute absence of the receiver or of any empirically determinable collective of receivers.'[10] In contrast to Austin who saw repetition as related secondarily to an original and valid event in its proper context, Derrida proposed that the written code presumes the absence of the recipient, as well as the sender, such that 'the written sign carries with it a force that breaks with its context . . . This breaking force is not an accidental predicate but the very structure of the written text.'[11] A written text is disengaged, then, from the writer, from the intended recipient and the intended context such that it exists validly and indeed in reality in many different contexts; so what is distinctive about the repetition of the text in an act of worship? This issue can usefully be explored through the functions of convention and context.

Convention

Convention, that is unspoken and implicit agreement, dictates that when we use the liturgical text in acts of worship it functions as legitimate prayer. However inadequate as an explanation, the conventions are established by consensus agreement among the participants; and we might interpret changes of denomination and congregation as indications of where the consensus has broken down. Canon law may also be brought in to sustain the convention, asserting which text and which authorized person may legitimately speak or do certain things, but even here a communal consensus

---

[10]Ibid., p. 7.
[11]Ibid., p. 9.

may outweigh that. Thus, it is not unheard of for some Anglicans to celebrate the Eucharist using the *Roman Missal*, a context not intended or authorized by either church, and for the worshippers to legitimize the event by their participation.

The congregation implicitly acknowledges this convention at the Sunday service, and understands that any prior preparations – rehearsals of hymns, readings, intercessions or ritual – are not the same thing at all. One would be reluctant to say that the latter were 'imperfect', or even 'infelicitous', as they may well be 'perfect' in that the performance of them in rehearsal may reach the level of what is hoped for in worship; but even so we do not accord the rehearsal the same value as the 'real thing'. When the worship begins there is a distinct change in focus and in expectation: the community anticipates divine presence following Christ's promise that, 'where two or three are gathered in my name, I am there among them'.[12] In terms of the text nothing has changed, but this context adds something which the other contexts do not possess – an anticipation of divine presence and encounter. In the rehearsal, or the classroom, the aim and focus is quite different, namely the refinement of the performance or the application of an interpretative method; these aims are not entirely abandoned in worship, but it seems that there is also the potential for meaning to be generated and found independent of our cognitive faculties and efforts. And we would argue, this is not just because of the communal nature of worship, the rehearsal and classroom are also communal contexts, but because the agreed convention about the use of the liturgical text during worship is the anticipation of divine presence.[13]

Context

Although Christianity has its holy places and shrines, there has never been an understanding of God's exclusive presence in them and hence 'context' as a validating prerequisite for the liturgical text is problematic. It is obvious that worship using liturgical

---

[12]Matthew 18.20.

[13]Such anticipation of divine presence and activity is explicitly asserted by, for example, the liturgical greeting 'The Lord is Here/ His Spirit is with Us' or the invocations of the Holy Spirit.

texts, indeed using the very same liturgical text, may occur in very different contexts and although some might be inappropriate, the nudist beach for example, none specifically invalidate the action or exclude the anticipated encounter. A baroque church, with professional choir and elaborate ritual may enhance the text but between that and a 'low mass' celebrated without music and with minimal personnel and ritual, there is no essential difference in the potential generation of meaning or potential encounter with the divine: both events are facilitated by the same text and that text also 'controls' the effects.

The variability of context goes hand in hand with the issue of repeatability: as with Derrida's assertion about all texts so with a liturgical text, repetition is built into textuality. Textuality disengages a communication from its context and enables it to be heard/read in any other conceivable context. Similarly, as liturgical texts are designed to be repeated they can never be specific to one particular context. With repetition the text is always the same and always different which means that also built into it is the potential to generate more or less meaning, for it to be more or less effective and this variability may be 'infelicitous' but it is normal. For the worshippers there will be sufficient, or even very close, resemblance to the previous time it was used to enable successful participation (i.e. use of the text), but worship will never be identical and the meanings derived from it may change.

Repetition in the liturgy

The discussion so far has been about the repetition of texts in a rather imprecise manner, but applicable to specific liturgies such as the Eucharist or morning prayer; however, even within a single liturgical event there can be repetitions of the same text and this leads us to observe that not all repetitions carry the same value, function and meaning. We can categorize three types of liturgical repetition: first, and most obviously, there is the repetition of liturgical events – Eucharistic liturgies, daily offices; secondly, of liturgical units – regularly occurring prayers, collects, blessings, etc.; and thirdly, of individual exclamations during the course of a single act of worship – 'Lord have mercy'. In every case the repetition neither adds to, nor erases, the previous occurrence. Worshippers do not repeat them in the hope that one day they will get it right, but each occurrence is complete in itself and contains the very same potential for meaning and encounter. The repeated element is incomplete because it is unfulfilled, not because it was previously invalid or inadequate. Let us look at a few examples of the second and third types and then discuss an anomaly.

In many acts of worship there is the repetition of a communal prayer of confession. Whether recited with full conscious participation or not, we can assume that worshippers are not being insincere, or merely pretending to confess their sins, or lying; however, they say these words knowing that in the next day or week they will repeat them. The subsequent recitations do not call into question the sincerity of the former and neither do they accumulate in force to imply that less and less needs to be confessed as time goes by. Logically the fulfilment of this text is by a complete reorientation of the worshipper's life so that he no longer sins, but theologically the Fall makes that impossible in this life, albeit the effects are mitigated by Christ's atonement. Textually and ritually, the confession is fulfilled, or completed, by the absolution, such that the deferred promises of forgiveness are actualized each and every time these two are recited. The repetition of the confession is not because of increased culpability but because repetition is, we have argued, part of the very nature of (liturgical) textuality; interestingly and conversely one would be unlikely to argue that the repetition of the absolution, given by the priest in God's name, indicates an imperfect absolution the previous time round. The communication of meaning (i.e. confessing one's sins) is not defective, nor is speaker's intention, rather it is built into the structure of this type of prayer text, that because of human sinfulness, as a post-lapsarian ontological condition, the text will be required to be repeated. We would suggest that repetition presumes incompleteness not invalidity.

A very different example is the Easter greeting 'Christ is risen/ He is risen indeed' used in different liturgical events, even repeated between the same people in the same liturgical event, between Easter and Pentecost. What sort of statement is it? It does not precisely fit Austin's definition of a 'constantive' statement as its function is not to convey a fact, even if it is believed to contain one; nor is it 'performative' as it does not effect that of which it speaks. Christ is no more risen from the dead by the repetitions than he is if it were uttered only once, the speakers do not acquire or increase their belief in the resurrection by its repetition, repetition does not add to its semantic meaning, nor does it invalidate previous recitations. Unike the 'Jesus Prayer', it does not correspond to the command to 'pray without ceasing' (1 Thessalonians 5.17), nor like the Sanctus does it correspond to a duty of praise. This statement contains a very restricted semantic meaning and its constant repetition would therefore seem to be superfluous or even frivolous and that indeed is sometimes how it is used. At an Orthodox Easter Vigil a common sight is the priests and deacons leaving the sanctuary one after another to go through the people censing them and frequently shouting out 'Christ is risen'. There is an element of fun in this ritual, but to call a repetition like this 'frivolous' is not to diminish it, rather it alerts us to the fact that its meaning is more than simply its semantic content.

There is one anomaly, though. A liturgical expression which has no efficacy if repeated in conjunction with the accepted ritual actions: the baptismal formula, 'I baptize you in the name of the Father, the Son and the Holy Spirit'. This statement is valid only once; to repeat it is to question not just the validity of the statement but of the divine gift and grace given by it. Thus, although it is possible to repeat the words with the actions, the repetition has no force and is invalid. Divisions between Christian denominations over when is the most appropriate time for baptism have occurred precisely because it is unrepeatable – thus some reject the validity of the words uttered at a previous event because the conditions for validity were not present, normally cognitive assent by the candidate, but they would still assert that there can only be one valid use of the words and ritual.

Textuality and participation

Liturgical revision of the last fifty years has been predicated upon the idea of the 'fully conscious and active participation' of all the people of God in the act of worship.[14] Essentially, this has been achieved by the provision of new texts in which the laity's role has been enhanced by speaking, acting and in devolved liturgical ministries. However, despite the increased opportunities for participation, neither the laity nor the clergy speak with their own words in the liturgy, but use the liturgical texts where their words, and to an extent their relationships, have been scripted. Although the term 'agency' is a fluid one,[15] it can here best be used to refer to the intentional and self-willed action, including speech, of an individual when participating in liturgical worship using an authorized text. We assume (or hope) that worshippers are 'agents' in this sense, although as the investigations of modes of participation will show, agency may be deferred or suspended, especially when divine agency takes precedence.

In much the same way as we explored in the chapter on authorship, where we found it helpful to distinguish the different processes by which a text came into being following Harold Love's taxonomy, here too it is helpful to identify a number of different 'participant roles'. A more developed understanding of who is participating and under what conditions focuses our attention on the multiple agencies operative in liturgical action. Webb Keane usefully summarizes:

> Erving Goffman . . . distinguished several roles involved in speech events, including the *principal* who bears responsibility for what is said, the *author* who formulates the actual words, the *animator* who utters them, the *proximal addressee* of the utterance, the *target* to whom the words are ultimately directed, and the *overhearer*.[16]

---

[14]*Sacrosanctum Concilium* 14: 'Mother Church earnestly desires that all the faithful should be led to that fully conscious, and active participation in liturgical celebrations which is demanded by the very nature of the liturgy.' <http://www.vatican.va/ archive/hist_councils/il_vatican_council/documents/vat-il_const_19631204_sacro-sanctum-concilium_En.html> [accessed 30 April 2013].
[15]See L. M. Ahearn, 'Language and Agency', *Annual Review of Anthropology* 30 (2001), pp. 109–37.
[16]Keane, 'Religious Language', p. 58 (author's italics), citing Erving Goffman, 'Footing', idem., *Forms of Talk* (Oxford: Basil Blackwell, 1981), pp. 124–59.

Applying these useful categories to liturgical worship, we note that Goffman starts 'behind the scenes', as it were, and forces us to acknowledge some unseen participants who control the words and actions through the liturgical text, even though they do not perform it. He places 'author' second, although we might prefer to place this function first to reflect the order of production, noting again that we have identified a number of 'author functions' in relation to liturgical texts. For many churches the *principal* could be identified as the synods and committees which authorize the text for use in worship. Assigning a role to the 'principal' also challenges us to reflect upon the overt influence of these bodies in the churches. It is these groups which act as a check on the creative activities of the 'author' and determine what potentially may be said and done in worship through rubrics and canon law. Some potential meanings are already in place, therefore, before even the book is opened and they are independent of the active participants in the liturgical act.

Thus as we turn to look at the roles played by these active participants we are aware that their agency, that is their autonomous activity, is already circumscribed. The *animator* utters the words in worship; the choice of the term 'animator' further alerts us to the limited agency in this role. Usually, the animator will be the priest and other ministers, although occasionally the people might also occupy this role. Animators bring the text to life according to their aptitude – how the words are voiced (where the emphasis falls; whether they are spoken or sung), what sort of gestures accompany them, what posture is adopted and what space they occupy when speaking. Animators dominate the liturgical event and their meaning of the text can be imposed through the physical performance of it, whether they are fully aware of it or not.[17] Their other role is to facilitate or direct the remaining active participant roles.

Goffman proposed a diffused 'recipient function' in the speech event: the *proximal addressee*, who is actually present; the *target* to whom the communication is directed; and the *overhearer*. These roles are not fixed, but shift and merge between the human participants who are present in the liturgical event and God as the liturgy unfolds. Thus the congregation are clearly the proximal addressee and the target when called to confess their sins, but are

---

[17]See Hughes, *Worship as Meaning* where he proposes one methods of investigating how the animator's 'signs' are received by the worshippers.

overhearers when the priest recites the Eucharistic prayer which is directed to God; they are the target of the prayer of absolution even though this is addressed to God, but the proximal addressees of blessings which are only indirectly addressed to God. What the liturgical reforms of Vatican II achieved was to move the people's role from being almost exclusively that of overhearers, to enable them to fill these other roles and even to act as animators in certain circumstances, and this was achieved by changes to the liturgical text.

There is though a further unintended consequence of this distribution of roles in the ritual event, as Keane notes, in that as the principal and author of the text are not present or when divine authority for the text and action is assumed, it displaces responsibility for what is said and done away from those immediately and physically involved in the event.[18] When speaking from a liturgical text, the autonomy and intention of the speaker becomes ambiguous: to what extent can scripted prayer be authentic speech? Historically, and to the present day, answering this negatively is a feature of some Christian traditions who reject liturgical texts and prefer forms of prayer which the minister may write or extemporize for each act of worship.[19] Keane notes the tendency in religious language to shift responsibility for what is said away from the participants actually present:[20] for those using a liturgical text onto the authorizing body and for those rejecting a text onto divine inspiration. Either way the result is the same: a 'decentering of discourse'[21] in which the autonomy, agency and intentions of the speakers are either ambiguous or suspended entirely. However, those defending the use of a liturgical text have also asserted divine inspiration, as we can see in Jeremy Taylor's 1649 defence of the Book of Common Prayer written as a response to the (Westminster) *Directory for Public Worship* (1644). He rejected the immediacy of extempore speech because there was an insufficient gap between

---

[18]Keane, 'Religious Language', p. 59.
[19]An influential historical example is the so-called Westminster *Directory for Public Worship* of 1644 where set forms of prayer are deemed to limit the minister's exercise of his spiritual gifts. For a contemporary discussion of this issue see, for example, Chris Ellis, *Approaching God: A Guide for Worship Leaders and Worshippers* (Norwich: Canterbury Press, 2009).
[20]Keane, 'Religious Language', pp. 52–3.
[21]Ibid., p. 53.

thought and speech, whereas co-operation with the Holy Spirit in prayer required the use of deliberation and learning. He promotes the closeness of speech and writing in worship:

> In making our Orations and publike advocations, we must write what we meane to speake, as often as we can; when we cannot, yet we must deliberate, and study; and when the suddennesse of the accident prevents both these, we must use all the powers of art and care . . . that we be not destitute of matter and words apt for the imployment.[22]

The issue of agency and intention of the human participants, and the active role and validation of the Holy Spirit in the content of worship, was a key issue in this ideological conflict of the seventeenth century and it still echoes in the churches today.

The 'decentering' does not simply assert divine agency, but also provides the participants with authority for their words and actions based on tradition. As Keane has noted:

> The action being performed by a rite is, in principle, not created anew by the performers. Its efficacy depends on being accepted as an instance of something that can be repeated, and that cannot be derived solely from the speaker's intentions. One reason that some ritualists insist they are merely following the procedures laid down by ancestors is precisely to stress that link, forged by linguistic means, between an absence of intentionality on their part, and efficacy due to more distance (sic) powers.[23]

Social relationships

A further issue highlighted by a consideration of how the liturgical text affects participation concerns how the text creates social relations in the worshipping community through verbal and non-verbal means, and how these map onto theological ideologies of

---

[22]Jeremy Taylor, *An Apology for Authorized and Set-forms of Liturgie* (1649). <http://anglicanhistory.org/taylor/apology.html> [accessed 30 March 2013].
[23]Keane, 'Language and Religion', np. <http://www.blackwellreference.com/sub-scriber/tocnode.html?id=g9781405144308_chunk_g978140514430822> [accessed 31 July 2013].

the Church expressed in metaphors such as the 'Body of Christ' or the 'Communion of Saints'.[24] The liturgical scholar Mark Searle remarked that the words are not 'bits of information transmitted to God', but that 'While not devoid of semantic content, they are first and foremost utterances that involve and commit the participants in relation to one another, to Christ and to God.'[25] If the liturgical performance models the whole Christian life lived in relation to God in Trinity, represents the Church, militant and spiritual, to the people present at the event and to the world, then it is no surprise that it also models relationships. Linguistic anthropologists have emphasized 'language as social action', and consider 'language, whether spoken or written, to be inextricably embedded in networks of sociocultural relations.'[26] Thus, in the liturgical event who speaks, how dialogues function, who gives and receives sacramental elements, all these mirror social relations and the hierarchy in the community and, again, this is achieved independently of the semantic meaning of the words spoken from the text. Even the presentation of the text on the page can imply social relations in worship as we discussed in the previous chapter. And because the language of the liturgical text is so unlike normal speech patterns, the participants are alerted to different types of social relations which they simultaneously act out and acquire. A clear example would be the introductions to the exchange of peace at the Eucharist. The most common is:

We are the body of Christ.
In the one Spirit we were all baptized into one body.
Let us then pursue all that makes for peace
and builds up the common life.[27]

Or, that suggested for use on All Saints' Day:

We are fellow-citizens with the saints and of the household of God,

---

[24]See Gordon Lathrop, *Holy People: A Liturgical Ecclesiology* (Minneapolis: Fortress Press, 2006 [1999]).
[25]Mark Searle, *Called to Participate. Theological, Ritual, and Social Perspectives* (Collegeville: Liturgical Press, 2006), p. 53.
[26]Ahearn, 'Language and Agency', p. 110.
[27]*CW*, p. 290.

through Christ our Lord, who came and preached peace
to those who were far off and those who were near.[28]

These declarations are almost invariably followed by:

The peace of the Lord be always with you
All: and also with you.
Let us offer one another a sign of peace.[29]

In both introductions a statement is made about the identity of
the participants: they are the 'body of Christ', 'one body', 'fellow
citizens . . . of the household of God'. These indicate different social
relations than might be evident outside the context of worship,
or rather they may be true theologically, but may not be much in
evidence at the parish meeting. They function to state the reality
of the distinctive relations of the baptized to each other and to
God, but also through the ritual exchange of peace the participants
practise this relationship so that it might become a reality outside
the liturgical context as well. The difference between the liturgical
and everyday contexts must have been even more marked when
participants were expected to exchange a kiss of peace and not just
a handshake. In the Jerusalem liturgy from the late fourth or early
fifth century the deacon greeted the people with these words:

Greet one another; let us kiss one another.

The bishop goes on to explain, 'Don't take this kiss to be like the
kiss friends exchange when they meet in the market place. This is
something different; this kiss expresses a union of souls and is a
plea for complete reconciliation.'[30] Again the words, in their ritual
context, express distinctive social relations because in Roman
culture a kiss would never be publically exchanged with anyone
from a different social class.

---

[28]Ibid., p. 324.
[29]Ibid., p. 175.
[30]Cyril (or more likely John) of Jerusalem, *MC* 5.3. Translation in Edward Yarnold,
Cyril of Jerusalem (London and New York: Routledge, 2000), p. 182. See also, L.
Edward Phillips, *The Ritual Kiss in Early Christian Worship*, Alcuin/GROW Joint
Liturgical Study 36 (Nottingham: Grove Books, 1996).

The example of the peace is the most obvious in many respects as it is expressly about relationships, but there are other examples throughout the liturgy – in the content of the intercessions, the recitation of the creed, in the ritual of receiving communion. To the experienced participant these relations are so embedded in their expectation of worship that they probably go unremarked, only to arouse shock when encountering a differently ordered community when worshipping in another church.

Edward L. Schieffelin proposed that the social relations of the participants was more important than any meaning conveyed in a performance: 'Performance does not construct a symbolic reality in the manner of presenting an argument, description, or commentary. Rather, it does so by socially constructing a situation in which the participants experience symbolic meanings as part of the process of what they are already doing.'[31] The liturgical text hints at the relational, it makes new relationships possible, but for it to be effective the participants are required to enagage ritually, imaginitively, and we would say by experience, to complete the meanings only partially conveyed through the text and ritual; they are required to 'complete the construction of reality'.[32]

Textual worship and meaning

Discussions about the generation and appropriation of meaning in worship in recent decades have tended to concern themselves with what might be called a democratizing of meaning to emphasize that the authority behind the liturgical text does not monopolize or uniquely determine what it means and that the worshippers may take and generate unexpected meanings by their participation in the very same event. This is in part the conclusion of Martin Stringer, that meaning resides in the mind of each worshipper and that it is primarily inaccessible.[33] However, were we to ask a worshipper what a liturgical event, or text, meant to them we might well find

---

[31]Edward L. Schieffelin, 'Performance and the Cultural Construction of Reality', *American Ethnologist* 12, no. 4 (1985), p. 709.
[32]Ibid., p. 721.
[33]Stringer, *Perception*, p. 2 and elsewhere.

them reluctant to say what they think it 'means' because they may
assume that we are asking them to provide an exegesis of the text,
to give a theologically correct answer or simply because they do
not have the vocabulary and concepts to investigate and articulate
what it means to them; they will, though, be able to express that it
is 'meaningful'. As all this suggests the problem we have is that we
really have no idea what it is that we are asking when we say 'what
does (this) worship mean?' As Paul Horwich says of the similar
problem in philosophical discussions of 'meaning':

> One of the more easily avoidable sources of confusion in this
> area is that the word 'meaning' is deployed ambiguously, both
> in ordinary language and by theoreticians, to pick out various
> related but different phenomena. An expression's 'meaning'
> may be the concept it standardly manifests, or else the thing in
> the world to which it refers, or the propositional element that
> (given the context) it expresses, or what the speaker (perhaps
> mistakenly) takes it to be about, or what the speaker intends his
> audience to infer from its use.[34]

In liturgical studies, this ambiguity is abundantly evident in the
variety of interpretative methods which have been employed to
investigate the meaning of worship. Generations of seminarians
have been taught the 'meaning' of the liturgical text by an analytic
method focusing on the semantic meaning of the words, revealed
particularly by examining the historical context in which they
first appeared.[35] With the advent of ritual studies, more recent
seminarians are more likely to be taught that rituals contain meaning
and that these can be 'read' and analysed.[36] The hermeneutical
theories of Paul Ricoeur and Hans Georg Gadamer have enabled
analyses of the way in which meaning is generated from the text
in its performance, and thus what is there to be appropriated or

---

[34]Paul Horwich, *Meaning* (Oxford: Clarendon Press, 1998), p. 3.
[35]For example, nineteenth- and early twentieth-century manuals on the *Book of
Common Prayer* such as Francis Proctor's, *A New History of The Book of Common
Prayer with a Rationale of its Offices* (Cambridge: Macmillan, 1855), which was
revised by Walter Frere and went through multiple editions, the last being in 1961.
[36]See the essays collected together to function as an introductory textbook in Paul F.
Bradshaw and John Melloh, *Foundations in Ritual Studies: A Reader for Students of
Christian Worship* (London: SPCK, 2007).

'understood' by the worshipper.[37] Or, as Graham Hughes, in his excellent *Worship as Meaning*, Charles Pierce's semiotic theory is used to explore how meaning is generated in different ways during the liturgical event according to the type of sign-making employed, and that interpretation or understanding requires a collaboration between minister and worshipper. And in this book, yet another way of approaching the meaning of worship is proposed, which is that the text in the worshippers' hands will reveal meaning through its textuality and that this either disregards or supplements the semantic content and ritual context.

In analysing the textuality of our liturgical texts in the previous chapters, we have become aware that there are two independent processes going on in relation to meaning-making. First, the author expresses their meaning in the text through the words, genre, the construction of the narrative or through intertextual elements. The author's expression of meaning is both facilitated and constrained by these means: concerns such as faithfulness to tradition, adherence to doctrinal orthodoxy, the dominance of the biblical narrative and liturgical conventions all restrict the author's independent creativity, even before one brings in factors such as multiple authorship and the work of revision and authorizing committees. Unlike poetry or plays, the author is not autonomous in the meaning-making process and this is also due to the intended context in which the text will be used, where the expectations of the intended users, developed in turn by the worship conventions of their church, exercise a control which must be set alongside the particular features which the text's use in an oral context requires. Nevertheless, despite these constraints on the author's autonomous creativity, one would still want to assert that the liturgical text contains a set of intended meanings determined by an author understood in the broad way we outlined in Chapter 2. The author's control of the meaning is fixed at the point of the text's publication, notwithstanding supplementary notes and rubrics and 'General Instructions'; the author's control

---

[37]See, Bridget Nichols, *Liturgical Hermeneutics: Interpreting Liturgical Rites in Performance* (Frankfurt am Main: Peter Lang, 1996); Martin Stringer, 'Gadamer and Hermeneutics', *Anaphora* 1 (2007), pp. 1–18; Joyce Zimmerman, *Liturgy and Hermeneutics*, American Essays in Liturgy (Collegeville: The Liturgical Press, 1998).

over the use and interpretation ceases once the text is used in its intended context.

Liturgical worship relies heavily on the words for the meaning, the worshippers borrow these words and by doing so trust that the author has provided authentic words for them to use. It is at this point that the second 'meaning-making' context is operative, that between the text and the readers or worshippers. This occurs independently of the author and, although the liturgical studies seminar may provide one location for interpretation, the primary interpretation occurs in the worship event itself. Now meaning-making is not in the controlled environment of textual production, but is in the mind of the worshippers individually and collectively in a way which is more difficult to discern. To a great extent there must be shared meanings which allow a particular group of people to gather and worship in a particular way. Individuals may not agree with each other, nor may they always agree with the unspoken communal meanings, but it must be that the benefit of consensus outweighs any desire for the assertion of subjective interpretations.

Worshippers approach the text from a completely different angle than authors; by and large, they are completely unconscious of the production and intentional processes behind the text in their hands. When actively reflecting on the meaning of what they say and do, there will certainly not be a consistent approach: the text might be used to validate pre-existing opinions, or worshippers may be open to new meanings which the text proposes, or they may be surprised by challenges to long-held views, or emphasis might be placed on the communal action over the words. These suggestions are not exhaustive. Many liturgical commentators, for example those on participation, or more recently during the 'translation wars' in the English-speaking Catholic Church, presume that worshippers hold either a complete indifference to the text (Martin Stringer barely mentions it in his study of worshipping congregations), or that they arrive *tabula rasa* to the text and the liturgical event, ready to have the official meaning of the text poured into them. Martin Stringer highlighted this dichotomy by asking whether 'meaning is to be found entirely within the texts of the liturgy' or whether 'the meaning of the rite is found primarily in the minds of those who attend'.[38] In reality, a more nuanced and complex picture emerges in which the worshippers permit their meaning-making to be guided by the text, just as they permit their prayers and praise to be directed by it, but at the same time at different points in the liturgy they will draw upon experience, teaching, intuition, the context and community to derive meanings which they may well not be able to articulate even as they assert meaningfulness in the activity. Literacy skills assist the appropriation of the meaning proposed by the text, but even in their absence meaningfulness is still discerned which does not imply that the non-literate, or those without the text in their hands, reject the text's authority to direct the community's worship and to act as a locus on meaning.

Conclusion: The threshold of worship

Joris Geldhof has drawn our attention to the liturgy's position as 'between' God and humanity suggested by the philosophical enquiries into the nature of being proposed by William Desmond. In particular he focuses on one element of Desmond's philosophy, that of 'metaxology', of 'the between', or 'porosity', or 'permeability', understood as follows: 'The 'between' means the middle between extremes, and can be said to stand at the crossroads of different ultimacies which 'from beyond' make their inward moves, so that they become 'observable' and, albeit always to a restricted degree, interpretable for the human mind or being.'[39] Desmond himself asserted that, 'addressing this other between, or letting oneself be addressed by what is communicated in and across it, is, I think, inseparable from the religious'.[40] Geldhof's preliminary examination of this notion in relation to the liturgy highlights how

---

[38]Martin Stringer, 'Situating Meaning in the Liturgical Text', *Bulletin of the John Rylands University Library of Manchester* 73 (1991), pp. 181–94.

[39]Joris Geldhof, 'The Between and the Liturgy: On Rendering W. Desmond's Philosophy Fruitful for Theology', in L. Boeve and Christophe Brabant (eds), *Between Philosophy and Theology: Contemporary Interpretations of Christianity* (Farnham: Ashgate, 2010), p. 93.

[40]William Desmond, 'Between System and Poetics', in Thomas F. Kelly, *Between System and Poetics: William Desmond and Philosophy after Dialectic* (Aldershot: Ashgate, 2007), p. 27, quoted in Geldhof, 'The between', p. 94.

it functions at the 'crossroads of a *catabatic* and an *anabatic* move. The first refers to a move from God towards the human race, with whom he established an alliance; the second is interpreted as the human response to this divine initiative and symbolizes an upward move.'[41] Geldhof argues that it is appropriate to apply the idea of 'permeability' to the liturgy because of the way it facilitates reconciliation between God and humanity, both establishing and maintaining that relationship.[42]

Although Geldhof does not discuss the liturgical text in relation to porosity, it is possible to see how the text has an essential role in facilitating the effects which he attributes to liturgy – namely, reconciliation between God and humanity. At the very least by analogy, the text functions in this intermediary way; it does not constitute the relationship, but is between the worshipper and their communication to God, and God's communication with the worshipper. Desmond's notions of porosity, permeability, between'ness all help to establish the liturgical text as something which is not the end in itself, but is the essential means by which the desired worship is achieved. In order not to confuse our (mis-)appropriation of Desmond's ideas for an entity, whereas he proposes this as an ontological condition, we will suggest the term 'threshold' as more applicable to something concrete which at the same time stands between.

A threshold marks out spaces as well as the zone of transition between them: it is a barrier but one which is permeable, porous and between. Because of its physicality, its rubrics and instructions, its proposition of appropriate responses to God and to other people, it requires the participants to pass over or through into God's presence, to a place where his image and likeness may be restored. The liturgical text does not remain outside while the worshippers cross over the threshold to engage in real worship, but rather it constitutes the threshold itself; it receives its proper identity only when used to facilitate this transition. We have noted already the non-worship contexts in which the liturgical text may be used and how students are not worshipping when they study the liturgical text in a seminar. As a physical threshold only becomes a threshold at the moment of crossing it, so with the liturgical text, when it

[41]Geldhof, 'The Between', p. 95.
[42]Ibid., p. 97.

ceases to be an object and takes on its true character of being between, or porous, or permeable does it achieve its true function. Just as a threshold may be crossed again and again, so too at each repetition the liturgical text effects a transition. And, as with our daily experience the threshold always remains to trip us up but is mostly unremarked, worshippers simultaneously acknowledge the text by permitting their relationship with God and the church to be directed by it, and rightly disregard it as being neither the focus nor the goal of their activities.

BIBLIOGRAPHY

Ahearn, Laura M., 'Language and Agency', *Annual Review of Anthropology*, 30 (2001), pp. 109–37.

Albrect, Daniel E., *Rites in the Spirit: A Ritual Approach to Pentecostal/ Charismatic Spirituality*, Sheffield: Sheffield Academic Press, 1999.

Allen, Graham, *Intertextuality*, London and New York: Routledge, 2000.

Austin, John L., *How to Do Things with Words*, 2nd ed., Oxford: Clarendon Press, 1975.

Barthes, Roland, (translated by Stephen Heath), *Image, Music, Text*, London: Fontana Press, 1977.

—, 'From Work to Text', idem., *Image, Music, Text*, pp. 155–64.

—, 'The Death of the Author' [first published in French in 1968], idem., *Image, Music, Text*, pp. 142–8.

—, 'Theory of the Text', in Robert Young (ed.), *Untying the Text: A Post-structuralist Reader*, London: Routledge and Keegan Paul, 1981, pp. 31–47.

Bassnett, Susan, *Translation Studies*, London and New York: Routledge, 1991.

Bennett, Andrew, *The Author*, Abingdon: Routledge, 2005.

Book of Common Prayer, 1549. <http://justus.anglican.org/resources/bcp/1549/BCP_1549.htm> [accessed 29 July 2013].

—, 1552. <http://justus.anglican.org/resources/bcp/1552/BCP_1552.htm> [accessed 27 March 2012].

—, 1662. <http://www.churchofengland.org/prayer-worship/worship/book-of-common-prayer.aspx> [accessed 29 July 2013].

Botte, Bernard, 'L'Eucologe de Sérapion est-il authentique?', *OrChr* 48 (1964), pp. 50–6.

Bouley, Allen, *From Freedom to Formula: The Evolution of the Eucharistic Prayer from Oral Improvisation to Written Texts*, Studies in Christian Antiquity 21, Washington: Catholic University of America Press, 1981.

Bradshaw, Paul F., 'Liturgy and "Living Literature"', in Paul Bradshaw and Bryan Spinks (eds), *Liturgy in Dialogue: Essays in Memory of Ronald Jasper*, London: SPCK, 1993, pp. 138–53.

—, *The Search for the Origins of Christian Worship: Sources and Methods for the Study of Early Liturgy*, 2nd ed., London: SPCK, 2002.

Bradshaw, Paul F. (ed.), *A Companion to Common Worship*, vol. 1, Alcuin Club Collections 78, London: SPCK, 2001; vol. 2, Alcuin Club Collections 81, London: SPCK, 2006.

Bradshaw, Paul F. and John Melloh, *Foundations in Ritual Studies: A Reader for Students of Christian Worship*, London: SPCK, 2007.

Bray, Gerald L., *Language and Liturgy*, Latimer Studies 16, Oxford: Latimer House, 1984.

Brehaut, Ernest, *Gregory of Tours: History of the Franks*, New York: Norton, 1969. <http://www.fordham.edu/halsall/basis/gregory-hist. asp#book3> [accessed 27 March 2012].

Brightman, F. E., 'The Sacramentary of Serapion', *JTS* 1 (1900), pp. 88–113, 247–77.

—, 'The Anaphora of Theodore', *JTS* 3 (1930), pp. 160–4.

Bugnini, Annibale, *The Reform of the Liturgy 1948–1975*, Collegeville: Liturgical Press, 1990.

Capelle, Bernard, 'L'Anaphore de Sérapion. Essai d'exégèse', *Le Muséon* 59 (1946), pp. 425–43.

Church of England, *The Alternative Service Book*, London: Church House Publishing, 1980.

—, *Common Worship: Services and Prayers for the Church of England*, London: Church House Publishing, 2000.

—, *Common Worship: Pastoral Services*, London: Church House Publishing, 2005.

—, *Common Worship: Ordination Services*, London: Church House Publishing, 2007.

Church of Ireland, *Book of Common Prayer*, Dublin: Columba Press, 2004.

Church of Scotland, *The Liturgy of John Knox received by the Church of Scotland in 1564*, Glasgow: University Press, 1886. <http://archive.org/ stream/liturgyjohnknox00knoxuoft#page/146/mode/2up> [accessed 30 March 2012].

Connolly, R. H., *The Liturgical Homilies of Narsai*, Texts and Studies 8, Cambridge: Cambridge University Press, 1909.

Crites, Stephen, 'The Narrative Quality of Experience', in Hauerwas and Jones, *Why Narrative?*, pp. 65–88.

Crystal, David and Derek Davy, *Investigating English Style*, London: Longman, 1969.

Cuming, Geoffrey J., 'Thmuis Revisited: Another Look at the Prayers of Bishop Sarapion', *TS* 41 (1980), pp. 568–75.

Cuming, G. J., 'Pseudonymity and Authenticity, with Special Reference to the Liturgy of St John Chrysostom', *Studia Patristica* 15 (1984), pp. 532–8.

Cunningham, Mary B. and Pauline Allen (eds), *Preacher and Audience: Studies in Early Christian and Byzantine Homiletics*, Leiden: Brill, 1998.

Day, Juliette, *The Baptismal Liturgy of Jerusalem: Fourth and Fifth Century Evidence from Palestine, Syria, and Egypt*, Aldershot: Ashgate Publishing, 2007a.

—, 'Stories of Self and Salvation at Baptism', *Anaphora* 1, no. 2 (2007b), pp. 37–52.

—, 'Liturgical Authorship', *Anaphora* 3, no. 2 (2009a), pp. 39–56.

—, 'The Origins of the Anaphoral Benedictus', *JTS* 60 (2009b), pp. 193–211.

—, 'Interpreting the Origins of the Roman Canon', *Studia Patristica* 71 (2013), pp. 53–67.

De Saussure, Ferdinand, *Course in General Linguistics* [3rd ed., Charles Bally and Albert Reidlinger eds; translated by Wade Baskin] New York: Philosophical Library, 1959. <http://openlibrary.org/books/OL23291521M/Course_in_general_linguistics> [accessed 27 March 2012].

Derrida, Jacques, 'Signature Event Context', idem., *Limited Inc*, Evanston: Northwestern University Press, 1988, pp. 1–23.

Directory for Public Worship, The, 1644. <http://www.epcew.org.uk/dpw/> [accessed 27 March 2012].

Dix, Gregory, *The Shape of the Liturgy*, 2nd ed. repr., London: Continuum, 2001 [1945].

Drews, Paul, 'Über Wobbermins "Altchristliche liturgische Stücke aus der Kirche Aegyptens"', *ZKG* 20 (1900), pp. 291–328, 415–41.

Duchesne, Louis, *Christian Worship: Its Origin and Evolution*, 5th ed. translated by M. L. McClure, London: SPCK, 1923.

Duffy, Eamon, 'Rewriting the Liturgy: The Theological Implications of Translation', *New Blackfriars* 78 (1997), pp. 4–27.

Eizenhöfer, Leo, Petrus Siffrin and Leo C. Mohlberg., *Liber Sacramentorum Romanae Aeclesiae Ordinis Anni Circuli* (Cod. Vat. Reg. Lat. 316/ Paris Bibl. Nat. 7193, 41/56) (*Sacramentarium Gelasianum*), Rome: Herder, 1960.

Ellis, Christopher J., *Approaching God: A Guide for Worship Leaders and Worshippers*, Norwich: Canterbury Press, 2009.

Ellis, Christopher J. and Myra Blyth (eds), for The Baptist Union of Great Britain, *Gathering for Worship: Patterns and Prayers for the Community of Disciples*, Norwich: Canterbury Press, 2005.

Episcopal Church, The, *The Book of Common Prayer*, New York: The Church Hymnal Association, 1979. <http://www.episcopalchurch.org/sites/default/files/downloads/book_of_common_prayer.pdf> [accessed 21 August 2013].

Fenwick, John F., *The Anaphoras of St Basil and St James: An Investigation into their Common Origin*, Orientalia Christiana Analecta, 240, Rome: Pontificium Institutum Studiorum Orientalium, 1992.

Foucault, Michel, 'What is an Author?', in Josué Harai (ed.), *Textual Strategies: Perspectives in Post-structural Criticism*, London: Methuen, 1979 [1969], pp. 141–60.

Fowler, Alastair, *Kinds of Literature: An Introduction to the Theory of Genres and Modes*, Oxford: Clarendon Press, 1982.

Frow, John, *Genre*, London: Routledge, 2006.

Geldhof, Joris, 'The Between and the Liturgy: On Rendering W. Desmond's Philosophy Fruitful for Theology', in L. Boeve and Christophe Brabant (eds), *Between Philosophy and Theology: Contemporary Interpretations of Christianity*, Farnham: Ashgate, 2010, pp. 87–97.

Genette, Gérard, *Paratexts: Thresholds of Interpretation*, Cambridge: Cambridge University Press, 1997.

Goffman, Erving, 'Footing', idem., *Forms of Talk*, Philadelphia: University of Pennsylvania Press, 1981, pp. 124–59.

Hänggi, Anton and Irmgard Pahl, *Prex eucharistica. Volumen I: Textus e variis liturgiis antiquioribus selecti*, Fribourg: Éditions Universitaires, 1968.

Hauerwas, Stanley and David Burrell, 'From System to Story: An Alternative Pattern for Rationality in Ethics', in Hauerwas and Jones, *Why Narrative?*, pp. 158–90.

Hauerwas, Stanley and Gregory L. Jones (eds), *Why Narrative? Readings in Narrative Theology*, Grand Rapids: Eerdmans, 1989.

Hebblethwaite, David, *Liturgical Revision in the Church of England, 1984–2004*, Alcuin/GROW Liturgical Study 57, Cambridge: Grove Books, 2004.

Hillborn, David, *'The Words of our Lips': Language Use in Free Church Worship*, London: Congregational Memorial Hall Trust, 1998.

Hirsch, E. D., *Validity in Interpretation*, New Haven: Yale University Press, 1967.

Horwich, Paul, *Meaning*, Oxford: Clarendon Press, 1998.

Hughes, Graham, *Worship as Meaning: A Liturgical Theology for Late Modernity*, Cambridge: Cambridge University Press, 2003.

Hughes, Kathleen, 'Prayer, Types of, in the Liturgy', in Peter E. Fink (ed.), *The New Dictionary of Sacramental Theology*, Collegeville: The Liturgical Press, 1990, pp. 959–67.

Hymns Ancient and Modern, New Standard, Norwich: Canterbury Press, 1983.

Iona Abbey, *Worship Book*, Glasgow: Wild Goose Publications, 2001.

Irwin, Sara H., 'The Religiophenome: Liturgy and Some Uses of Deconstruction', *Worship* 80 (2006), pp. 234–52.

Irwin, William, *Intentionalist Interpretation. A Philosophical Explanation and Defense*, Contributions in Philosophy 73, Westport: Greenwood Press, 1999.

Jasper, Ronald C. D. and Geoffrey J. Cuming, *Prayers of the Eucharist: Early and Reformed*, 3rd ed., Collegeville: Liturgical Press, 1990.

Jauss, Hans Robert, 'Theory of Genres and Medieval Literature' in David Duff, *Modern Genre Theory*, Harlow: Longman, 2000, pp. 127–47.

Johnson, Maxwell E., *The Prayers of Sarapion of Thmuis: A Literary, Liturgical and Theological Analysis*, Orientalia Christiana Analecta 249, Rome: Pontificium Institutum Studiorum Orientalium, 1995.

Jungmann, Joseph A., *The Mass of the Roman Rite, Its Origins and Development*, translated by Francis A. Brunner, London: Burns and Oates, 1959.

Justin Martyr, *Apology*, in A. Cleveland Coxe, James Donaldson and Alexander Roberts (eds), repr. *The Ante-Nicene Fathers: Translations of the Writings of the Fathers Down to A.D. 325*, vol. I: *The Apostolic Fathers* Grand Rapids, MI: Eerdmans, 1985, pp. 424–518.

Keane, Webb, 'Religious Language', *Annual Review of Anthropology*, 26 (1997), pp. 47–71.

—, 'Language and Religion', in Alessandro Duranti (ed.), *A Companion to Linguistic Anthropology*, Oxford: Blackwell Reference Online, 2005. <http://www.blackwellreference.com/subscriber/tocnode. html?id=g9781405144308_chunk_g978140514430822> [accessed 31 July 2013].

Ladrière, Jean, 'The Performativity of Liturgical Language', *Concilium* 9, no. 2 (1973), pp. 50–62.

Lathrop, Gordon, *Holy People: A Liturgical Ecclesiology*, Minneapolis: Fortress Press, 2006 [1999].

Linde, Charlotte, *Life Stories: The Creation of Coherence*, New York: Oxford University Press, 1993.

Long, Lynne (ed.), *Translation and Religion: Holy Untranslatable?*, Clevedon: Multilingual Matters Ltd, 2005.

Lord, Albert B., *The Singer of Tales*, 2nd ed. revised by Stephen Mitchell and Gregory Nagy, Cambridge, MA: Harvard University Press, 2001 (1960).

Love, Harold, *Attributing Authorship: An Introduction*, Cambridge: Cambridge University Press, 2002.

Lyotard, Jean-François *The Postmodern Condition: A Report on Knowledge*, translated by Geoff Bennington and Brian Massumi, Minneapolis: University of Minnesota Press, 1984.

MacIntyre, Alasdair, *After Virtue: A Study in Moral Theology*, London: Duckworth, 1985.

Martyn, John R. C., *The Letters of Gregory the Great*, 3 vols, Toronto: Pontifical Institute of Mediaeval Studies, 2004.

Milavec, Aaron, *The Didache: Faith, Hope and Life in the Earliest Christian Communities, 50–70 C.E.*, Mahwah, NJ: Newman Press, 2003.

Mingana, Alphonse, *Commentary of Theodore of Mopsuestia on the Lord's Prayer and on the Sacraments of Baptism and the Eucharist*, Woodbrooke Studies 6, Cambridge: Heffer, 1933.

Morley, Janet, *All Desires Known*, 3rd ed., London: SPCK, 2005.

Nichols, Bridget, *Liturgical Hermeneutics: Interpreting Liturgical Rites in Performance*, Frankfurt am Main: Peter Lang, 1996.

Nida, Eugene A., *Towards a Science of Translating*, Leiden: Brill, 1964.

O'Loughlin, Thomas, *The Didache: A Window on the Earliest Christians*, London: SPCK, 2010.

Ong, Walter, *Orality and Literacy: The Technologizing of the Word*, London: Routledge, 2002.

Origen, *On Prayer*. <http://www.ccel.org/ccel/origen/prayer.xxi.html> [accessed 29 March 2012].

Palazzo, Eric, *A History of Liturgical Books: From the Beginning to the Thirteenth Century*, Collegeville: Liturgical Press, c. 1998.

Phillips, L. Edward, *The Ritual Kiss in Early Christian Worship*, Alcuin/GROW Joint Liturgical Study 36, Nottingham: Grove Books, 1996.

Plett, Heinrich F., 'Intertextualities', idem., *Intertextuality*, Research in Text Theory 45, Berlin and New York: de Gruyter, 1991a, pp. 3–29.

Plett, Heinrich F. (ed.), *Intertextuality*, Research in Text Theory 45, Berlin and New York: de Gruyter, 1991b.

Podmore, Colin, 'The Design of *Common Worship*', in Bradshaw (ed.), *Companion*, vol. 1, pp. 255–9.

Prince, Gerald, 'Reader', *The Living Handbook of Narratology*, Hamburg University Press, 2011. <http://hup.sub.uni-hamburg.de/lhn/index.php/Reader#Definition> [accessed 29 March 2012].

Proctor, Francis *A New History of The Book of Common Prayer with a Rationale of Its Offices*, Cambridge: Macmillan, 1855.

Ramshaw, Gail, 'The Pit, or the Gates of Zion? A Report on Contemporary Western Liturgical Language', *Worship* 75, no. 1 (2001), pp. 12–19.

Ricoeur, Paul, 'What is a Text?' idem., *From Text to Action: Essays in Hermeneutics II*, translated by Kathleen Blamey and John B. Thompson; London: Athlone Press, 1991, pp. 105–43.

Riffaterre, Michael, 'Compulsory Reader Response: The Intertextual Drive', in Worton and Still, *Intertexuality*, pp. 56–78.

Ritivoi, Andreea Deciu, 'Identity and Narrative', in Herman, D., Jahn, M. and Marie-Laure Ryan (eds), *Routledge Encyclopedia of Narrative Theory*, London: Routledge, 2005, pp. 231–5.

Roman Catholic Church, *Sacrosanctum Concilium* (1963). <http:// www.vatican.va/archive/hist_councils/ii_vatican_council/documents/ vat-ii_const_19631204_sacrosanctum-concilium_En.html> [accessed 26 March 2012].

—, *Comme Le Prévoit* (On the translation of liturgical texts for celebrations with a congregation, 25 January 1969). <http://www. ewtn.com/library/CURIA/CONSLEPR.HTM> [accessed 29 July 2013].

—, *Liturgicae Instaurationes* (Instruction on the orderly carrying out of the Constitution on the Liturgy, September 5, 1970). <http://www. ewtn.com/library/CURIA/CDWLITUR.HTM> [accessed 12 August 2013].

—, *Liturgiam authenticam* (2001). <http://www.vatican.va/roman_curia/ congregations/ccdds/documents/rc_con_ccdds_doc_20010507_ liturgiam-authenticam_En.html> [accessed 29 July 2013].

—, *Missale Romanum ex decreto sacrosancti oecumenici concilii Vaticani II instauratum auctoritate Pauli PP. VI promulgatum Ioannis Pauli PP. II cura recognitum, Editio typica tertia*, Vatican City: Typis Polyglottis Vaticanis, 2008.

—, *The Roman Missal*, English translation according to the Third Typical Edition, Dublin: Veritas, 2011.

—, *Eucharistic Prayers for Masses with Children*, for Use with the *Roman Missal*, 3rd ed., Dublin: Veritas, 2013.

Russell, Donald A., *Criticism in Antiquity*, 2nd ed., London: Bristol Classical Press, 1995.

Schieffelin, Edward L., 'Performance and the Cultural Construction of Reality', *American Ethnologist* 12, no. 4 (1985), pp. 707–24.

Searle, John R., *Speech Acts: An Essay in the Philosophy of Language*, Cambridge: Cambridge University Press, 1969.

Searle, Mark, *Called to Participate: Theological, Ritual, and Social Perspectives*, Collegeville: Liturgical Press, 2006.

Şerban, Adriana, 'Archaising versus Modernising in English Translations of the Orthodox Liturgy: St John Crysostomos in the 20th Century', in Long, *Translation and Religion*, pp. 75–88.

Spinks, Bryan, *The Sanctus in the Eucharistic Prayer*, Cambridge: Cambridge University Press, 1991.

Stringer, Martin, 'Situating Meaning in the Liturgical Text', *Bulletin of the John Rylands University Library of Manchester* 73 (1991), pp. 181–94.

—, *On the Perception of Worship*, Birmingham: University of Birmingham Press, 1999.

—, 'Gadamer and Hermeneutics', *Anaphora* 1, no. 1 (2007), pp. 1–18.

Tabouret-Keller, Andrée, 'Language and Identity', in Coulmas, Florian
(ed.), *The Handbook of Sociolinguistics*, Oxford: Blackwell Publishing,
c. 1997, pp. 315–26.

Taft, Robert, 'The Authenticity of the Chrysostom Anaphora Revisited.
Determining the Authorship of Liturgical Texts by Computer',
Orientalia Christiana Periodica 56 (1990), pp. 5–51.

Taylor, Jeremy, *An Apology for Authorized and Set-forms of Liturgie*
(1649). <http://anglicanhistory.org/taylor/apology.html> [accessed
30 March 2013].

Vogel, Cyrille, *Medieval Liturgy: An Introduction to the Sources*,
Washington, DC: Pastoral Press, 1986.

Wheatley, Charles, *A Rational Illustration of the Book of Common
Prayer of the Church of England: Being the Substance of Everything
Liturgical in Bishop Sparrow, Mr. L'Estrange, Dr. Comber, Dr Nichols,
and all Former Ritualists, Commentators and Others upon the Same
Subject*, London: Henry G. Bohn, 1848.

Wheelock, Wade T., 'The Problem of Ritual Language: From Information
to Situation', *JAAR* 50, no. 1 (1982), pp. 49–71.

Willis, Geoffrey G., *Further Essays in Early Roman Liturgy*, Alcuin Club
Collections vol. 50, London: SPCK, 1968.

Wimsatt, William K. and Monroe C. Beardsley, 'The Intentional Fallacy',
in W. K. Wimsatt (ed.), *The Verbal Icon: Studies in the Meaning of
Poetry*, Lexington, University of Kentucky Press, 1954, pp. 3–18.

Wobbermin, Georg, *Altchristliche liturgische Stücke aus der Kirche
Aegyptens nebst einem dogmatischen Brief des Bischofs Serapion von
Thmius*, TU 17 3b, Leipzig and Berlin: J. C. Hinrichs, 1898.

Worton, Michael and Judith Still (eds), *Intertexuality: Theories and
Practices*, Manchester and New York: Manchester University Press,
1990.

Yarnold, Edward J., *The Awe-inspiring Rites of Initiation: The Origins of
the RCIA*, Edinburgh: T&T Clark, 1994.

—, *Cyril of Jerusalem*. London and New York: Routledge, 2000.

Yates, Nigel, *Buildings, Faith and Worship*, 2nd ed., Oxford: Oxford
University Press, 2000.

Zimmerman, Joyce, *Liturgy and Hermeneutics: American Essays in
Liturgy*, Collegeville: Liturgical Press, 1998.

INDEX